GARDNER'S *guide to*

WRITING AND
PRODUCING
ANIMATION

SHANNON MUIR

GARTH GARDNER COMPANY

GGC publishing

Washington DC, USA · London, UK

Cover Designer: Nic Banks
Layout Designer: Rachelle Painchaud-Nash
Editor: Chris Edwards
Publisher: Garth Gardner, Ph.D.

Editorial inquiries concerning this book should be mailed to:
The Editor, Garth Gardner Company, 5107 13th Street N.W.,
Washington DC 20011 or emailed to: info@ggcinc.com.
http://www.gogardner.com

Library of Congress Cataloging-in-Publication Data

Muir, Shannon.
  Gardner's guide to writing and producing animation / by Shannon Muir.
      p. cm.
ISBN 1-58965-027-1

  1. Motion picture authorship. 2. Motion pictures—Production and
direction. 3. Animated films. I. Title.
  PN1996.M83 2006
  808.2'3--dc22   2006033104

Printed in Canada

TABLE OF CONTENTS

PREFACE

There are a lot of books on the market geared to those who want to draw for animation, and more recently titles focused on writing for the medium. However, next to nothing really existed on the market that addressed the other non-artist jobs in animation. That's why I began writing columns on the Internet trying to bring all I could on the subject to help fill what I perceived as a void that is now slowly being filled.

Having noted that the book's primary focus is on producing, as well as the production pipeline, there is a semi-detailed chapter on writing included in this book. This is not only because writing is a natural step in the production process, but writing for animation has always been my first desire. But the field is competitive and though I dreamed of getting the chance since my teenage years, it wasn't until 2003 that a Japanese company would give me an opportunity to write five scripts to be translated back into Japanese and marketed to an Asian audience. So before that opportunity, and while I wait for others, I did and continue to do the next best thing—write about the medium that I live and breathe and love.

Without the artists and animators, there can be no animation. Never lose sight of that. However, those who sketch cannot do their best work bogged down by the struggles of fashioning budgets, schedules, ensuring all models completed by deadline, and other aspects of an animated show getting made. That's where the non-artists come in. I personally believe that the relationship between the artists and non-artists on a project should not be antagonistic; that each side, should, in fact, help the other to create a high-quality product in the end. The reality is that this occurs a lot less often than it should, and sometimes the line between artist and non-artist can be very divisive.

"Non-artist" is a rather encompassing term I use for anyone involved with an animation project that does not draw any of the materials needed to create the show, such as layout, character sketches, or storyboards, in addition to key animation and in-betweens. A "non-artist," then, includes writers, story editors, voice actors, casting directors, post-production staff, line and associate producers, production coordinators, and production assistants. Non-artists also can be sheet timers, given they understand the principles of animation. It is worth noting that (possibly rightly, as it is not easy to master) there are some people that strongly feel only artists and animators should do this kind of work.

I have worked hard to try and eliminate any type of bias in this book and just present the facts about the business, and generally speaking, I feel I have done a good job. However, there are two realities I need to work against and it is possible to not have succeeded as well as I might have liked. The one reality is that as much as I respect artists, I am not one of them and can never completely walk in their shoes. The other comes from the fact I was trained by and largely employed by writer-producers in my career. Combined with my own strong interest in writing, I worry that I may come off with a bias against producers trained in art, and this is the furthest from the truth. Without artists there can be no animation, period. If an artist becomes a producer as well, and has the gift of story to go with it, all the better.

My hope is that this book appeals to a wide variety of people. The main audience of the columns, and by extension the book, is those who want to know how to get in to the business of producing in the animation medium. However, I also hope that people already in the business who do not regularly deal with some of the other areas featured in this book will learn more about our industry as a whole. The animation audience itself also, as shown through such things as DVD extra features on animated films, wants to know more about how things work "behind the scenes" and I feel a wealth of such information can be found here. One thing the book includes to support this is "spotlight interviews," where I ask for the take of another professional of the industry on several issues touched on in each chapter. Some chapters even have two or more such pieces because of the depth and breadth of the subject matter. I feel it very important to hear not only the viewpoint of other producers, but also the types of people a producer gets on his team in order to achieve a full picture. For those who read this and plan to put the knowledge into action, I recommend reading the whole book before proceeding, instead of doing each step at each chapter; this way you will clearly understand the entire process.

Always be aware that the business is horribly cyclic. As I'm writing this, times for animation are very lean. I've seen many of my friends not work for months. I myself have gone a long time between shows. When I first moved here in 1996, the industry clamored for any talent they could get. For a while it was impossible, then a boom happened again, and now it seems many studios are scaling back. Maybe things have improved again as you read this, or perhaps you'll be the one to blaze a new trail by striking out independently if things are in a slump.

I believe there can never be change if no one takes a risk and dares to hope.

Shannon Muir
Los Angeles, CA
August 2006

PART ONE:
It Begins With the Producer…
the Story… and the Money

CHAPTER ONE

So, What's a Producer Do Anyway?

THE NUMBER ONE QUESTION

The question leading off this chapter probably ranks as one of
the top questions in the business. Just read the credits to any
television show or movie. You will see titles such as Line
Producer, Associate Producer, Supervising Producer, Consulting
Producer, and Executive Producer… just to name a
few! Yet, it is common knowledge that without a
producer nothing gets made. Not to mention, there
are often many of these producers in different
capacities on various projects. Nowhere is any clue
provided as to what these people do. Then comes
the question, "which type of producer makes it
happen, or can any of them fill the role?" The
goal of this chapter is to sort out what the
various producer titles mean, and then clarify
the driving role to get projects made.

WHAT DOES A PRODUCER DO?

As stated above, the roles of a producer can differ for a variety of reasons.

SPOTLIGHT INTERVIEW

TAD STONES

Tad Stones worked at Disney for over 20 years in features and television before going freelance. His career began at Disney, entering the Feature Animation training program three days after graduation and after completing their training became an in-between on *The Rescuers*. Later, he moved into the story department on *The Fox and the Hound* and then transferred over to Walt Disney Television Animation as it began to ramp up. During his years with Television Animation, he became known for creating *Darkwing Duck*, and producing and/or story editing series such as *Chip 'N Dale's Rescue Rangers, Aladdin, Buzz Lightyear of Star Command*, and *Hercules*. Tad also produced the Disney direct to DVD features *Return of Jafar, Aladdin and the King of Thieves*, and *Atlantis 2: Milo's Return*. After Disney, Tad took on a new challenge in sharp contrast to his Disney credits as Supervising Producer/Director on the *Hellboy* animated features to DVD for IDT Entertainment. He shares his views on the role of producer.

"The producer is the voice of the production to management. He has to understand what they expect from his production and have a clear idea of why they put his project into production. If his series was ordered to be the big action foundation for a block of action figure/ toy based shows, it would not be a good idea to start experimenting with the comedy and 'girl appeal' of the series. Generally, a producer is hired because the studio or network likes his work so there shouldn't be a conflict of interests. I've found that the better the understanding of the desired goals of the network/studio up front, the more creative freedom I have in getting it done. This is not to say that you don't have to fight to keep a show on track in the face of an avalanche of network notes.

The producer is the creative lead...sometimes called 'the bottleneck.' All creative decisions are ultimately his responsibility. Usually he delegates certain creative areas to others: a director, an art director, story editor or writer, etc., but they should be chosen by the producer because they reflect his taste or the vision he has for the project. Usually he oversees them directly. The people a producer chooses for his crew is one of the most important, if not THE most important, decision he must make. Outside of the above, the producer is responsible for delivering the project on time and on budget. If the project absolutely needs more time or money, the producer is the one who makes the case to management.

My favorite programs have been those that gave me the most creative freedom. I try not to abuse the freedom because it leads to the same freedom on the next project. Specifically, my two top favorites have a personal appeal to me. *Darkwing Duck* was my tribute to the goofy, 'silver age' of comics when Jimmy Olsen, Superman's Pal, was turned into a turtle boy, a human porcupine, or a melon-headed genius of the future. *Hellboy Animated,* my current project, is something I've been trying to get animated for about ten years. It's the most adult project I've worked on and the most ambitious. The creative challenge is really exciting.

Aside from the pleasure that comes from creating any work of art, I enjoy putting together a group of people who interact creatively. I don't know that I'd enjoy the life of a solitary artist. I enjoy ideas being tossed back and forth and watching someone take something of mine, whether written or drawn, and taking it to a higher level.

It's not a job that you should set as a goal. What you want is the ability to put your creativity on the screen, no matter the size. "

WHAT AN ANIMATION PRODUCER IS NOT

Before we break into a more detailed discussion on animation producers, let us begin by discussing what things not to expect of an Animation Producer. An Animation Producer is not…

… necessarily an artist. True, animation is a visual medium. Yet, not all producers need to be able to draw to be effective. As long as there is a sense for art and its effective application in animation, and a good sense of story, and an understanding of animation timing, a non-artist stands a fair shot at being a decent producer.

… always a highly educated specialist in cinema, theatre, or business. Skills that can serve a producer effectively can be picked up in other trades and moved over provided the producer has a passion or dedication to what he or she does. A good example is one person I know of who ultimately became a line producer came from successful work in high-end clothing retail, and to the best of my knowledge she did not have an MBA. That said, knowing something about either the creative side of the business or the business of the business never hurts, but it is not a necessity in and of itself. Even those with cinema backgrounds didn't start out necessarily intending to be producers. I know of producers with acting backgrounds, and even one who started as a film editor.

… a "deity," "genie," or "magician" who can make production problems magically disappear. By this I do not mean just problems within the physical production pipeline, but between members of a crew. Production problems are real occurrences and cannot just be swept under the rug, so a producer needs to be able to minimize the impact of problems to keep the production quality to the highest standards possible. Having said that, others must realize that the producer cannot fix everything, and can at best act as a problem solver or mediator to try and keep everything flowing.

… incapable of making mistakes himself or herself. This sort of goes along with the statements in the prior point, but I separate it for a reason. It's very important to stress that the producer can as much be the source of a production problem as anyone else, he or she is not on a pedestal above reproach. That said, any mistake on a production, whether or not the producer's actual fault, will reflect on the producer and be his or her responsibility.

THE DIFFERENT KINDS OF ANIMATION PRODUCERS

There is a saying about there being about as many types of producers as flavors of ice cream, and it seems to be a fair comparison. One of the things that make it so complicated to determine who does what is that oftentimes titles are dictated by items such as contracts and seniority and less by actual amount of time or other investment in the production. Some producers only handle financial aspects, some strictly creative aspects, and in some smaller studios these may even combine. With that in mind, here is a breakdown of some of the most commonly encountered titles in television and film and what they might most likely be applied to, all else being equal and speaking in generalities (realize in this business there are always, if not oftentimes, exceptions):

Executive Producer – Generally, these are the producers who also serve as financiers of a project, or make the connections to have the money brought in. Sometimes their clout alone earns them this distinction. Also this title can be given to the individuals who run any work-for-hire studios the financiers hire, provided these people carry sufficient clout. Since these people are either bringing in the money or giving it themselves, the weight of their clout alone adds credibility to a production, or they serve to liaisons with those who contribute to the project, and this gives them more than a fair amount of power. Largely they just give notes on the process and are not usually hands on, but those notes do carry a lot of weight in regard to the production as a whole. In some cases, if it is simply a matter of an Executive Producer who has attached their name for reasons of clout, they may have little or no hands on involvement. This title could also in theory be bestowed upon producers who serve with the a television production for many years to differentiate their contributions and seniority status from other producers brought on board in later years; that would depend on the politics of a specific series.

Line Producer – Line Producers often handle the budgeting and financial aspects after the budget's approval by higher producers. They also serve as the primary contact for the production heads of any overseas teams, interface directly with any overseas supervisors working in the company's capacity, and liaison with others related to the production such as union representatives. In a television studio environment, sometimes they juggle several animated series and then have one Associate Producer (or Production Manager) below them who handles a series exclusively.

Supervising Producer – Generally seen in live-action television and in that case often given to Story Editors, this term could in theory be used in animation to promote a dedicated producer who has served several years on a series but does not yet have the clout for an Executive Producer title. I have also heard of Supervisory Producer as a similar alternate for this title.

Associate Producer – In most studios this role is equivalent to that of Production Manager, and in fact Production Manager appears to be the more frequent term used in animation these days. However, a few studios still do use the Associate Producer term. Basically, this individual tends to be put in charge of recruiting the freelancers, and handling the day to day routine management business of a production, while the financials, and the high-level contacts, are left in the hands of those above them. They report to a Line Producer who often oversees multiple shows. Many major actions, however, must still be done in concert with, or at least after consulting, the Line Producer.

Consulting Producer – Usually seen more often in live-action than animation (though I believe I have seen it used in prime time animation), and also generally restricted to television, the Consulting Producer tends to describe someone who played a larger producer role in past seasons of a series but for whatever reason currently does not interact with the project as frequently. Sometimes these producers are called on for advice on a project based on their past familiarity with a project's history, while other times the title is simply part of a contractual agreement and the person does not actively participate in any way.

Segment Producer – Use of this title appears to be virtually unheard of in animation. However, I thought I better point it out in case any readers hear the term and wonder about it. This term means just what it says, that this person produces a part of the overall product. Most often it is seen in news programming. I suppose it could be used on shows that are made up of both animation and live-action segments to keep the producers separate and distinct, but I cannot think of an actual case where this has been done. More than likely though, these producers would be identified by their segment type (e.g., Animation Producer, Live Action Producer).

The "plain vanilla" Producer – This one is probably the hardest of all to describe. Sometimes it truly is a matter of having so many producers on a show there needs to be set of basic standards that the others are built around in terms of seniority. In other cases, the shop is so small that this kind of producer may be the only type on board using a "jack of all trades" title.

DOES IT MATTER WHERE A PRODUCER IS BASED?

It is worth noting that the physical proximity of a producer to a production has no bearing on the level of effectiveness at which a producer can operate. I worked on a show where many of the producers (who also happened to be employees of the company that owned the creative property) worked out of the United Kingdom. All of them remained fairly involved in the process thanks to the influence of such things as email and FTP clients. Though they did come for occasional meetings, generally they worked from "across the pond" without a problem. There are also shows that have staff producers who maintain offices at the production facility, and freelance producers who maintain offices elsewhere and show up when and where they are required.

WHICH TYPES OF PRODUCERS HAVE THE MOST POWER?

On the surface, this question may seem really simple. Yet to answer it, one must first bear in mind that titles are very fluid and vary from production to production, so the best we can do here is speak in generalities. Then, it must be determined what the "power" is in reference to, because different producers have control over different areas. Those producers who hold those titles as financiers of the production hold power to dictate how and where the money is spent, as well as influencing creative content; this especially falls true in cases where a pre-existing property (e.g., toy, videogame) becomes the focus of an animation production, where executives from the company owning the pre-existing property serve as producers.

Associate Producers (a.k.a. Production Managers) tend to be very much involved in the affairs of individual creative talent. This is from matters as simple as timesheets to matters as complicated as hiring and firing. That said, generally speaking matters of having people start or end on a production must be done in consultation with an Associate Producer's respective Line Producer to make sure all proper protocols and courses of action (especially in the case of a union production) have been followed.

As pointed out previously, however, titles tend to be fluid. A producer with a title at one studio may have a completely different amount of authority and responsibility as one with the exact same title at another studio. So it is hard to paint a clear picture for every possible title in every possible circumstance.

WHAT MAKES A GOOD PRODUCER?

A few common traits emerge between producers despite some very diverse styles handling their shows. A good producer:

- **Clearly understands that animation is a series of steps:** This element comes as one of the top elements for an effective producer. Animation production does not compare to making a soup or stew from whatever just happens to be lying around the kitchen. It must begin with an outline, then a script that goes to storyboard or a storyboard with action and dialogue (with a voice recording if needed), then an animatic (storyboard edited to the audio track), to full-out animation, to post-production; even then, this imagery is very oversimplified as that will be seen reading further into the book. These steps cannot be done out of order or the quality of the production is compromised for all involved.

- **Has a good sense of story:** The knowledge of what makes a story flow effectively proves helpful at every stage in the game, because no matter how good something may look in its artwork, if the story fails to engage the viewer all the flash and show will more than likely wear off or never merit a second viewing. From needing to know if the plot points in the initial outline work, to knowing which scenes can be cut at the storyboard stage because they'll have the least impact on story, to even understanding how a few little edits to cut around problem finished animation can impact what takes place, knowing story is crucial.

- **Is a good multitasker:** A producer needs to juggle many things at once, particularly in the case of episodic series, where he or she can be handling 13, 26, or even more episodes at various stages of production. Some items may be in preproduction, others currently being animated off-site (usually overseas), and still others undergoing final audio or video edits to be prepared for air. To a lesser extent, this also holds true for feature film, as each of its various sequences that comprise the larger whole must be tracked.

- **Is a people person:** By "people person," I do not necessarily mean a highly social butterfly. But a producer needs to be able to deal with individuals, from those known well to complete strangers. He or she must be able to diplomatically handle a wide range of personality types, and make sure they can all get along well enough for the production to proceed to completion. They also must be able to interact with representatives from a variety of outside vendors that interact with the production, from overseas studios to post houses and more, depending on the producer's exact responsibilities.

- **Anticipates problem areas and solves problems appropriately:** Even the best maintained and well oiled machine can run into difficulties, and so too with an animated series or movie. They also may not occur at the same points from production to production. As a producer gets a feel of the capabilities of his or her staff, they should be able to sense weaknesses in the pipeline and be prepared to take action. An example would be being able to figure out in advance the appropriate time to hire a few extra freelancers in a brief crunch period when it becomes apparent that even at their top speeds, the existing crew will be completely unable to complete storyboard deadlines, and yet hire them in such a way that their time on the production means minimal additional expense. Failure to meet deadlines can completely grind a production to a halt at any stage of the game; that is why a producer needs to be on top of things.

- **Sees things from all sides and prioritizes:** When the overseas studios, prop artists, and post house all hit a producer at once with various issues, the producer needs to be able to see things not only from his or her studio's perspective but be able to "walk in the shoes" of whomever the producer deals with. This does not mean always be sympathetic and give in to the others who have demands, but a producer at least needs to understand why the others feel their demands to be as important as they are. Maybe it's a case of inflated self-importance, or maybe the issues are legitimate; in many cases, these other vendors juggle other shows besides the one the producer is on and the issue with the producer's production affects others at their shops. It is up to the producer to discern and sort this out to the benefit of the production first and foremost, pleasing the various vendors as the producer is able.

A type of person whose opinions can serve as a barometer of an effective producer is the executives from studios, networks, and other venues who deal with producers on a regular basis.

SPOTLIGHT INTERVIEW

SANDER SCHWARTZ

Sander Schwartz currently serves as President of Warner Bros. Television Animation. Previously, he worked as President of Columbia-Tristar Children's Television (later known as Sony Animation and also known as Adelaide Productions). He shares his idea of an effective producer.

"An effective Producer will have the ability to motivate his/her crew and to inspire them to do their best work. Strong leadership and organizational skills are also paramount. The role of the Producer as to the production is the same as that of a conductor to an orchestra. The Producer must plan the project from beginning to end…and oversee it from inception to completion. The most important thing for the Producers to pay special attention to in order to make the production run smoothly is to make sure to hire the right people for the right jobs. Nothing is more important than choosing staff wisely.

The best advice I have to offer hopeful Producers is to be prepared to take any job that will provide relevant experience and add weight to one's resume."

GOING FOR IT

Now to those brave souls who still wish to embark on this adventure, congratulations! One may or may not make a lot of money doing this, and it will be hard work (though, hopefully, more a labor of love than anything else). There will be tough experiences as well as easy times, some very long days and other rather short ones. Unpredictability runs rampant in the entertainment production business, animation as much as anywhere, and one has to be ready and willing to "go with the flow" whatever is required. The result can be a chaotic mess, or absolutely wonderful, but a lot of that depends on how the producer handles himself or herself. In other words, if one steps into the producer role, the ending of this story will largely be up to that person.

SUMMING IT ALL UP

A producer's role can be as diverse as the variety of producer titles in existence. Generally speaking, a producer shepherds others working on the project, whether it is to get funds, meet deadlines, or keep the production process flowing. Producers must be able to handle a lot and see a problem from all sides in order to head off potential problems. Having said that, be aware that producers are not magicians who can solve any issue that comes along, and are not above reproach. The job is tough, demanding, but also potentially very rewarding for someone who loves the animation business.

CHAPTER TWO

What Should You Produce?

SOME THINGS TO CONSIDER BEFORE BEGINNING

"Dos" and "Don'ts"

DO… make sure a property is something you are passionate about and can stay strongly committed to. If you choose a concept thinking it will excite others and make money for you when you really don't care about the idea, the attitude will ultimately show through, and it will only make it that much harder to sell. This especially applies if it isn't a property with the strongest of "high concepts" or "hooks" but has other merits. How can anyone else believing in coming on board alongside that producer as a financier, staff person, or distributor if he or she is not strongly behind it at all stages of the project?

DON'T… consider something simply because it appears to be the kind of thing selling right now. Remember that it takes time to get something made. There are probably several similar shows already in the pipeline. By the time your idea would hit the market, the craze may well be over. That even assumes one can get far enough to be funded and produced. People may already think there are too much of the current hot properties out there. A producer must develop a sense of thinking ahead of the curve, of things that will have that "hook" or unusual appeal. This can be great visuals, strong characters, whatever. A lot of it is gut instinct, unfortunately; there is no real "magic formula."

DO… make sure the rights are available to something before proceeding. One of the biggest horror stories I hear is people embarking on adapting their dream book, toy, whatever, and then finding out they cannot do it because they cannot get permission from the rights holders. This does not mean do not consider pursuing it, but do it correctly. If the property is something you are passionate about, at least do the research and find out who holds the rights. If it isn't a concept many are clamoring over, the rights holder could very well be thrilled to hear from a potential producer and something might work out, but that's not always a guarantee. Without trying, one will never know. In short, if you cannot obtain the permission, forget about it.

DON'T… rely completely on flash over substance when considering what to produce. Remember, whatever one ultimately does, the property needs to go the distance regardless of what it is. If you are considering a television series, it has to run over the course of more than just a few episodes and stay fresh and interesting enough that people keep want to be tuning in. Even a feature film, while it doesn't have to scream that a sequel is necessary, should make people finish it wanting more and provide a logical outlet for there to be more (whether it be a sequel movie, follow-up television series, whatever is most appropriate and feasible). If nothing else, the property needs legs for marketing and merchandising so you can make the most of your investment. Flash will initially get them interested in whatever one has to sell, but without substance that will very likely fizzle quickly.

DO… get a clear picture of what type of animation the project should be before things begin to come together. While it is true that many 3D computer generated images (also known as CGI) films have done very well, films such as *Curious George* show that 2D cel animation (such as that used in classic Walt Disney features) isn't quite dead yet, and the Academy Award winning *Wallace and Gromit* feature film illustrates the popularity potential for less common animation formats such as claymation. What type of animation a producer selects for a project will dictate the budget needed, the expertise and size required of the crew, and that one chooses a story that can be told in that form, among other factors.

Union or Non-Union (That is the Question)

At first, this seemed to me like it belonged in the "Financing, Scheduling and Budgeting" chapter (see Chapter 4), but the more I reflected on the subject, it seemed optimum to have this consideration in mind as one selects what property to work on. This thought largely stems from the fact that one needs to know what caliber of people envisioned to be working on a dream project, and if a producer is willing to become signatory to a union to make it happen. Better to rule out a project at this stage than budget the production, find one cannot afford the union talent and will not compromise for less, and then scrap it after wasting not only time and energy but those who bid on the project. Also, if one does want to have a union shop, there will be certain arrangements that need to get into place before crewing up, not to mention the effect on budget.

One may be wondering what is so important about unions and the benefits of being signatory. A way is that the union serves as an invaluable direct connection to accessing experienced talent, especially since all the major studios use the union as their talent base. Unions also provide a standardized way to deal with health and pension benefits as those covered by the unions earn points by working with a company versus a producer handling this on their own. The flip side is that the unions dictate the minimums that one can pay people in each of these categories, and others issues on their members' behalf when dealing with a production. Below I will describe the history and importance of unions in the United States of America, since this is where I work. Hopefully this will allow readers in other parts of the world to form the needed questions to make the proper local inquiries.

It is important to note that the history of union work and animation can be a bit complex and the full history beyond the scope of this book. In the United States, The Animation Guild 839 (one of many unions under the umbrella of IATSE) began life in 1952 and was known for many years as the Motion Picture Screen Cartoonists Guild. Every major studio belongs to this guild, some such as Disney and Warner Bros. Dating back to the early years and others like Nickelodeon joining more recently. In the mid 2000s, MPSC merged with a guild handling optical electronic and graphic arts, and the new name of The Animation Guild 839 is the result (though most people in the industry call it simply 839). If a production is 839, this will cover nearly its entire staff—production personnel such as assistants, coordinators, managers, and producers are excluded.

Where this does create some confusion, at least at the time this book is going to press, comes in the area of writers. When most people think of writers, they think of scripts, and in turn might assume that the writers are also excluded and instead covered by the Writers Guild of America. This is not the case in 839 shops, where the writers are part of the covered personnel. The origin comes out of the fact that animation scripts did not come into regular use until the rise of Hanna-Barbera in the 1970s; before that, story points were written in conjunction with the board and these individuals were known as "storypersons" which received coverage under 839.

However, that is not to say that the Writers Guild of America (WGA) does not cover animation. At this writing, all prime-time broadcast network animation gets WGA coverage, which came about after a work stoppage of all of the writers on the hit prime-time animated series; many of these writers came from the live-action sitcom environment and because of this were accustomed to that union and its benefits. Even the prime time series *Father of the Pride,* made by 839 shop Dreamworks Animation, ended up having to negotiate a compromise so that its writers (who also came from the live-action sitcom world) would have to get some WGA union contributions. So if one plans to produce for prime-time, know going into it that one may have to consider WGA union coverage for writers. There are some additional things attached here such as the concept of residuals (the writer receiving additional payments when the show re-airs the first few times, foreign airings, and other special situations).

The WGA also provides the ability, through the Department of Organizing, and specifically the Animation Writers Caucus, to negotiate to get individual writers covered by the WGA even if the animation production itself is otherwise non-union. This is good to be aware of whether there is a specific writer one wishes to pursue that will only work with a WGA contract, or alternatively, if a writer one wants to work with asks for this kind of arrangement. These arrangements can apply to animated television or film. As of this writing, the main things involved are making sure the writers' health and pension are paid. Residuals can, but do not always, apply in these cases at the time I write this.

The other major exception to be aware of involves the voice actors. Voice actors are not handled by 839 in the United States, but are under the Screen Actors Guild. Unless one does a completely non-union production, there will be Screen Actors Guild actors in the cast, and one must be ready to pay them accordingly. Dubbing foreign animation (discussed later this chapter) also tends to be Screen Actors Guild covered as well, so do not automatically assume that if one wishes to produce this type of programming one will run a non-union shop. Screen Actors Guild contracts include additional things not previously mentioned such as residuals (additional payments) that kick in when an episode is rerun, airs in foreign markets, etc. similar to the Writers Guild of America as mentioned above.

All that said, one can still go completely non-union, as I said above, but the biggest limit this puts on a producer is that one then cannot hire anyone who belongs to one of the above listed unions. The upside is that there are no restrictions on the wage minimum one can pay the workers on the production. That said, being non-union puts strict limits on the talent pool from which one can draw which could be a serious drawback.

OPTIONS FOR WHAT CAN BE PRODUCED

Developing One's Own Concept

At first this seems like the simplest approach, to just completely come up with someone on the producer's own. It eliminates any worry about the rights issues as previously discussed, as a producer does not need to negotiate with anyone and retain full ownership of the idea. However, if one is not able to properly format and flesh out the needed development documents on his or her own (to be discussed in detail in Chapter 3, "Focusing on the Story"), a producer then needs to be able to go through the process of finding someone to do this for him or her. That person will need to understand a producer's vision and be able to translate it in an exciting, informative way that will excite potential investors, additional writers a producer may want to bring on board (for a television series especially), etc.

Seeking Out a Concept to Produce and Develop

There are two major routes to seek out concepts to produce and develop that do not originate from a Producer's own development: taking pitches from other creators about their previously un-produced concepts, or finding an existing property and produce it as animated project.

The process of taking pitches can be very time consuming. In a nutshell, this involves people coming to the Producer and "selling" why their idea deserves to be an animated project. First, a Producer needs to get the word out that ideas are being solicited. Many only allow ideas to be submitted through agents or managers to help keep some kind of control process on the flow, as there will be so many people eager to see if the Producer can help them be "the next big thing." Some people may ask the Producer what he or she looks for, and the best thing is to have a response ready that is in line with the "do"s and "don't"s from earlier. Otherwise, a lot of precious time of the Producer's – and the presenters – may very well be wasted. More specific details on pitching can be found in Chapter 3, "Focusing on the Story," to be used in situations where Producers do their own development on a property (whether self-created or refining one that rights have been acquired to) and then pitch it to financiers or others with the ability to greenlight, or approve, an animated project. Pitches can be done with or without concept art to accompany a pitch; see Figures 2.1 to 2.6 for examples of concept art.

COPYRIGHT 2006 KEVIN PAUL SHAW BRODEN

Figure 2.1 Lineup of Concept Characters

Figure 2.2 Concept Art Depicting Characters in Action

Figure 2.3 Concept Characters in Poses

Figure 2.4 Female Concept Character Pose

Figure 2.5 Male Concept Character Pose

Gardner's Guide to Writing and Producing Animation

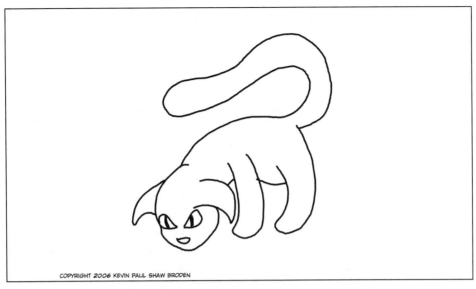

COPYRIGHT 2006 KEVIN PAUL SHAW BRODEN

Figure 2.6 Animal Concept Character Pose

Seeking out a pre-existing property also takes a lot of time and effort, because instead of the property ideas coming to the Producer, the Producer goes and looks for the properties. A Producer needs to stay abreast of what is available on the market. Examples range from books, toys, videogames, comics, websites, and clothing, just to name a few possibilities. There are a variety of ways in which to research these options. In today's times, surfing the web can make a lot of the research easier but it definitely isn't the sole method. Trade shows and conventions are crucial to the property search, spending more time at the smaller booths and independent tables than the big name areas. It may even mean attending shows focusing on areas a Producer may not have gone to in the past, such as a convention of independent book publishers.

Offering Services to a Company to Produce a "Work-For-Hire"

While similar to a scenario where a producer seeks out an existing property, in this case, a company that owns a property does development on a property but a partnership with a studio does not yet exist. The company that owns the property hires the producer (and the crew that producer will help bring on board) to oversee the implementation of their pre-existing development. A special note to this is that no pre-existing studio infrastructure would be in place and a producer likely would be involved to some degree with establishing this framework.

Coming on Board to Produce a "Work-For-Hire" Project for Someone Else

This kind of scenario occurs when a production company already possesses previously assembled development materials and needs to take on a producer for this project to shepherd it through the process. In this case, the producer is being brought into an existing studio with many resources already in place. While this takes some pressures off a producer, it also limits the producer's involvement.

Producing Dubbed Foreign Animation

With the growing mainstream popularity of importing foreign animation in recent years (such as the anime explosion in the United States), and interest in other properties from around the world growing, a potential producer may be tempted to or have the connections to bring in a property from another country and produce it for their home market. The first thing to be keenly aware of is that this is a completely different process that does not precisely follow the pipeline as laid out in this book. Basically, since the animation already exists, a producer in this area will go through some elements of Pre-Production and generally will skip to the Post-Production stage (except for the rare cases where new, original animation has to be created for editing purposes). Otherwise most of the early and late steps are relatively similar.

The major difference with dubbing foreign animation comes from the fact one starts out with pre-existing animation; one does not have to invest money designing models or getting finished animation from overseas. The bulk of the work comes in the form of editing the picture to standards suitable for the audience and area of the world a producer would wish to target, then laying down what is called visual timecode on this video without sound. The video, along with a very literal translation of the Japanese dialogue (which one will have to invest time and expense to have done) get passed out to writers who come up with natural sounding dialogue to fit the mouth and preserve as much as possible the essence of the original dialogue. The exception to this is if your goal is to use the foreign video and massively change the underlying story, in which case one will have to take the costs of developing providing some sort of writer's guide to the staff. After the scripts are written, new dialogue tracks are recorded and edited to picture, and then the original M&E (music and effects) tracks are mixed back in with the new dialogue for the finished product.

SPOTLIGHT INTERVIEW

MARC HANDLER

Marc Handler has over 20 years of experience in foreign animation production as a writer, story editor, and voice director. His credits include both television and feature film. Marc is best known for his dub work on the anime favorite *Cowboy Bebop* television series and its feature film, as well as other fan-favorites such as *FLCL* and *Tenchi Muyo*. He also worked as a writer and story editor on *Voltron: Defender of the Universe*. He shares some of his experience working on dubbed productions.

"It's harder to write for a show that needs a lot of re-editing. Of course, most of the time it's not that extreme, they're just cutting out violence and such, things that just can't be aired on US television, and as a writer you have to try to smooth it out so it doesn't seem chopped up—keep the narrative as clear and smooth as possible. In addition to these American problems, a lot of time you're working on shows where the original production in Japan was badly planned and thrown together in the first place. So, in those cases, you're trying to take weak stories and strengthen and clarify them. I was in a story meeting in Tokyo, and some of the animators told me very candidly that it's rare for the production teams they work with to pay much attention to story. They put most of their energy into the animation, and in many cases that has to be done very fast on a very slim budget. The writers only get paid half of what American writers get, even though Tokyo is more expensive than any American city—so the writers work very fast, doing lots of shows at the same time. The result is that some series have serious writing problems with long digressions, big gaps in the narrative, etc. We try to fix and clarify those things wherever possible, but it's often an uphill fight.

It's a real joy when you get to work on a series like *Cowboy Bebop*. Here it's clear that the creators have given careful attention to each detail of the story, the animation, and every aspect of the production: the result is very high quality stories and a superb overall production. I have immense respect for Keiko Nobumoto who story edited that series, as well as Shinichiro Watanabe, Yoko Kanno, Sadayuki Murai, and the many other people who worked on *Bebop*. We did not re-edit a single frame of the *Bebop* series or film, we studied the episodes carefully, and worked very hard at staying as close to the original as possible. That does not mean going with a direct word-for-word translation—the old phrase "lost in the translation"—is apt—if you use direct translations in anime, much is lost, often the essence of the scene. Anime fans who believe they are getting "real authentic anime" when they read subtitles are deluded. The Japanese version is usually colorful and full of life, but the subtitled/ direct translation is typically flat and lifeless because the life, the spin, the color of the language has been lost in the translation. So my challenge is to take the content of the translation, then bring it back to life by bringing the mood and texture of the scene into the dialogue. I really enjoy that challenge because, with an excellent series like *Bebop*, the end result is terrific. You can enjoy watching it and feel good about it, and you know there are lots of fans out there who appreciate it when you do it right."

SUMMING IT ALL UP

Though it is good and important to pick a project one is passionate about, also be sure to research that rights to a property are available and decide early on what type of animation the project should be. Don't just follow what is currently "hot" or "a hit" or choose a product with limited storytelling potential. Also it needs to be determined early on by the producer if he or she wishes it to be a union or non-union project as certain arrangements may need to be put into motion before you can even open up shop. Options for what can be produced include: developing one's own concept, acquiring an existing marketed property to adapt into animation, taking 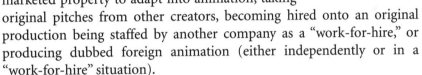 original pitches from other creators, becoming hired onto an original production being staffed by another company as a "work-for-hire," or producing dubbed foreign animation (either independently or in a "work-for-hire" situation).

CHAPTER THREE

Focusing on the Story

WHY SHOULD A PRODUCER CARE ABOUT WRITING?

Without writing, there is nothing to produce. Period.

That is not to say all animation starts in the hands of scriptwriters, though much of it does; some of it is done by storyboard artists who also provide the dialogue. Some animation gets produced with no dialogue at all and it is all about the visuals.

But under it all is a story, and a story must be written.

Overall, however, one must bear in mind that regardless of the approach, the discussion involves items ultimately intended to use as tools to sell a property that other creative or financial partners are recruited to help support. This advice does not apply to, and this book is not intended to explore, creating samples to obtain work for hire employment. Also, this chapter only discusses the steps and structure of development and writing, but not the craft, which is far beyond the scope of these pages.

HOW ARE SCRIPTS FORMATTED?

These days, almost all scripts are done on the computer. Specialized script formatting programs such as *Final Draft* (Final Draft, Inc.), *Movie Magic Screenwriter* (Write Brothers, Inc.), and *Scriptware* (Cinovation) will be the way scripts are passed around for editing and reading, though they may be printed as required by cast and crew. For those more intimately familiar with the formatting layout of a script or who cannot afford the specialized programs, a set of macros in Word format will do just as well provided they are to the proper specifications. Even if the producer does not intend to write the script, the producer will need to be able to read what the writer submits. Some of the specialized programs do make free reader programs (for reading and printing only) available, and this may serve a producer's needs. Specifics on how to format a script are beyond the scope of this text.

THE DIFFERENCES BETWEEN ANIMATION AND LIVE-ACTION WRITING

Truthfully, there aren't many differences at all. A story is still a story, the main issue here is that animation has been chosen as the medium with which to tell this particular tale. That said, animation tends to gear itself to stories that require a lot of action, since drawn "talking heads" are difficult to get excited about.

Compared to their live-action counterparts, animation scripts show some differences, though a prime-time animation script bears a much closer resemblance to its live-action sitcom counterpart, and some scripts are written exactly like live-action scripts in the case of 3D computer generated animated programs that write everything in "master shots" to leave everything up to the director. Since most producers reading this probably will not be gearing towards prime-time animation, and information about live-action script format is plentiful, most of the chapter's focus will be on the more common animation script format. The prime-time animation format will be illustrated briefly for comparison later on in the chapter.

HOW MUCH NEEDS TO BE WRITTEN DOWN TO SHOW INVESTORS?

Truthfully, no cut and dried formula exists here. The biggest factors are a producer's personal credibility in the business (i.e., how much people are willing to trust a producer without any hard evidence of a project as backup), a producer's strengths and weaknesses (what items can a producer make that will give the project's best presentation), and the business needs of the potential business partner or financier. More specific ways on how to utilize these items will be discussed in Chapter 4, "Financing, Scheduling and Budgeting," but this chapter will concentrate on how to produce these tools for getting the production off on the right foot.

Many ideas are sold on a bible or less. Some producers want to have the whole movie in hand before they approach others to fund the idea; if a producer goes this route, be aware that this is called writing on "spec," or speculation. This basically means one is writing the script for free upfront and then finding the financing. Many professional writers will not do this, so if this is how a producer hopes to get a movie made, the producer may very well be forced to do a first draft himself or herself and then pay a professional writer for rewrites after financing is obtained. A safer method might be a beat outline or treatment by the producer (to be discussed later this chapter) and then getting the financing to hire professional writers for the script based on the outline or treatment.

SHOULD A PRODUCER DO THE DEVELOPMENT OR HIRE SOMEONE?

This goes back in large part to the producer's credibility, along with strengths and weaknesses, as mentioned in the previous section. If the producer's reputation includes being a strong storyteller or world-builder, and the producer has the know-how to take those ideas and put them down clearly in acceptable industry formats, there is no reason the producer shouldn't do development work. However, many producers do not have these areas in their strengths and end up hiring the job out to others to flesh out their kernels of an idea, or of an idea the producer acquires rights to.

Then it becomes a question of who to hire. Factors here include finding someone whose body of work the producer respects, someone who has a good rapport with the rest of the animation (if not larger entertainment) community so the developer's credibility can also help sell the project, and also a good personality mix between producer and developer so everyone can stay in tune with the same vision.

SPOTLIGHT INTERVIEW

CHRISTY MARX

Christy Marx comes from years of experience in animation and related fields. While she is best known for her development work on the animated series *Jem,* Christy's extensive credits include writing *X-Men: Evolution, G.I. Joe, He-Man and the Masters of the Universe, Reboot, Conan the Adventurer,* and the first incarnation of *Teenage Mutant Ninja Turtles.* She's also written for live-action series including *Babylon 5,* computer games including the award-winning PC game *Conquests of Camelot* and its sister game *Conquests of the Longbow,* console games including *The Legend of Alon-Dar,* and the massively multiplayer online game *Earth and Beyond.* In 2000, Christy Marx received the lifetime achievement award from the Writers Guild of America for her contributions to the animation writing community. Here, she shares some advice on development.

"My first break was being hired to develop *Jem and the Holograms.* That came about because the people at Sunbow Productions loved the scripts I'd written for *G.I. Joe.* Basically, you become known for the type of thing you're good at writing, and I'm very good with action-adventure, science fiction, and fantasy. The first step is to get noticed by doing very good work. Then keep doing very good work.

I don't tend to make much of a distinction between adapting an existing property (like a comic) or 'expanding' an existing property (like toys). This is probably because I simply think of development as development. I can either have the world and characters there, as in a book or comic, or I can have a bit more freedom with toys where they may not have anything beyond the look of the toys and some basic concepts. Either way, the process of developing another property into an animation series requires sifting through whatever you have to determine what will work and discarding the rest. A good example of this was the *Conan* series. I reread every single one of Howard's *Conan* stories. I had a lot of background and a full rich world to draw upon, but

I still had to find a way to make a sword-wielding barbarian work in the world of children's animation where even the word 'kill' is generally not allowed. And I still had several characters to create that never existed in Howard's world, but existed as toys. From my point of view, it's a matter of degree, rather than one being radically different from the other situation.

Though no obligations whatsoever were made upon me when developing something like *Conan*, I personally feel I owe it to the creator and original writer to have respect for his or her work. It's a courtesy from one writer to another. Never mind that the other writer may have been dead for decades. It is the courtesy I would hope for should someone decide to adapt some work of mine decades after I'm gone. It's the least we can do.

I had to find the means for *Conan* to dispatch large numbers of enemies without actually killing anyone. Let me tell you, that is no easy feat. I gave him a sword made of meteorite metal that glows in the presence of the lizardmen and one touch from this star-metal sends the lizardmen into another dimension. *Poof!* No blood, no death, but lots of action. It may sound silly, but it's better than what they had to do with *Teenage Mutant Ninja Turtles* where we had to write martial arts characters carrying weapons that they can only use indirectly on inanimate objects, which is the other standard workaround for this type of action character. You have to make sure you please the client (the toy company) with what you do, and include any special notions or needs they toss at you. Beyond that, I think it's nothing but pure fun. I love having the freedom to create entirely new characters with nothing but a doll or a sketch to work from."

THE DEVELOPMENT STEPS

Bible

A "bible," sometimes referred to as a "series bible" or "show bible" in television, lays out the world of the animated series or feature film. It contains information about the main characters, common locations, plot guidelines, rules of the world (in cases where highly defined science or magic strongly influences the makeup of the series), and other pertinent information. The length varies depending on the needs of the series but all information within the bible must be presented as clearly and succinctly as possible. Once a series is in production, this information will be handed out to writers to keep them all "on the same page" as it were; yet a bible gets put to use as far back as the development stage as a primary development document. At any stage in the series life cycle the bible is intended to be a road map yet organically is open to change.

Here is an example of the opening pages of a series bible for a show called *Anything is Possible,* which I wrote up for a contest one of the major companies held a few years back for show development. Nowadays, I probably would have retitled it simply by virtue of the gangbuster success of the Walt Disney animated series *Kim Possible* to avoid any confusion of there being a spin-off connection, but for purposes of illustration only there isn't a point in pursuing a new title at this point (just be aware that if a person was still actively marketing a concept in this situation, a name change would be strongly recommended).

The premise of this show would be a show would best be described along the lines of *All Grown Up* (the *Rugrats* spin-off), *Rocket Power,* or *As Told by Ginger* where the stories aren't fantastical enough to need to be animated per se but certain quirky elements of the show play better in this kind of format. I'll be the first to argue that there might be far better examples to use, but this lends itself very well to allowing me to make a point later this chapter. See Figure 3.1 for a sample of the bible for this series.

ANYTHING IS POSSIBLE
Series Development by SHANNON MUIR

SERIES OVERVIEW

ANYTHING IS POSSIBLE follows five friends in 6th grade
beginning to find their way in potential careers. Each
tries a wide base of things in the same general emphasis
area, allowing for a wide variety of plot possibilities.
One week the characters go on an archaeology field trip and
the history buff's framed for breaking a fossil; another
week, one character's friends help him break through
creative blocks to finish an assignment instead of giving
into temptation to copy another's work. There's always a
problem involving what a character aspires to be and the
character and their friends figure out how to solve it.

This series lends itself to the animated medium because of
the child protagonists' flights of fancy as they
contemplate creative ways to tackle life's problems.
Ultimately a compromise comes about that must be real-world
and yet innovative, at times a combination of several
character's skills -- in hopes that the viewers will be
encouraged to tap their personal talents, engage in
problem-solving and encourage teamwork.

PROTAGONISTS

LYLIA - Lylia's interest lies in the sciences. She
experiments with physics, chemistry, biology, just to name
some areas. Personality-wise she's open and outgoing and
loves everyone. Her cousin is Rake, the visual artist.
Despite her science smarts, she's not "nerdy" in any way.

RAKE - Rake's into all forms of visual art, from painting
to pottery and more. Rake is particularly grumpy and
grouchy, but if you look past his exterior there's a kind
person underneath. He's dealt with a lot of rejection from
early in his life and built walls early. Rake's cousin is
Lylia the scientist, and it's possible his blood tie is the
only reason they let him hang around... Rake's attitude
certainly doesn't endear him to anyone.

KAYLI - She's got fantastic athletic ability. Will Kayli
become a track star, become a physical therapist, take up a
career as a nutritionist, or become a personal trainer?
Kayli's the shyest of the bunch and sensitive of everyone's
feelings.

Figure 3.1 – First page of bible for *Anything is Possible*

MATT - Matt, the musician, has the most "plain" name of the bunch. He wants to create something to be his stage name, but nothing ever seems to fit. Matt aspires to be a rock star, but who knows? He might find that he enjoys his first experience at a classical symphony, performing in musical theatre, or that actually being a recording engineer's more rewarding. Matt also composes music and writes lyrics... with mixed results.

ARMANO - Armano can easily be called a history buff. His nose is totally into geography, anthropology, not to historical periods like the Roman Empire to the World Wars. All of this fascinates Armano. He could easily be an investigative reporter, given his "in-your-face" assertive attitude. But maybe Armano would be happier as a cartographer, who knows?

ANTAGONISTS
JONNIE - The school bully, twin brother of J.M. He probably could be really brilliant at the sciences if he applied himself, Jonnie's smart enough to break videogame codes. Yet Jonnie would be lazy about life if his sister J.M. didn't know how to push his buttons.

J.M. - Twin sister to Jonnie, and the mastermind of this bully duo. J.M. (her real name's Juliet Meghan) enjoys breaking people down instead of trying to build herself up. J.M.'s smart and secretly enjoys writing, but she'd never dare tell. That's for nerds, and she wants to be cool.

Figure 3.1 – Second page of bible for *Anything is Possible*

To illustrate that the fundamentals of a show bible do not necessarily change when writing a prime-time show, just imagine that the show idea presented proved to be successful and years later a production company decides to revisit the same characters again, but this time instead of being in sixth grade they are just starting college.

Pay attention to what elements remain the same, and which ones differ. In particular, note that only a passing familiarity with the original series is assumed; this document may end up in the hands of people not familiar with the show. It must strive to present older information in a new way for those who know it, while "filling in the gaps" for those newer to the concept, all the while being able to stand on its own as an independent series pitch.

Take a look at the opening three pages of the show bible from *Anything is Possible: The College Edition,* which is featured as Figure 3.2.

ANYTHING IS POSSIBLE: THE COLLEGE EDITION
Series Development by SHANNON MUIR

SERIES OVERVIEW

As kids, they helped each other find their way in potential careers while living life. Now on their own in college, the cast of ANYTHING IS POSSIBLE work on fine-tuning their career paths with a formal college education... with a new friend and a whole new set of life lessons thrown into the mix.

Welcome to ANYTHING IS POSSIBLE: THE COLLEGE EDITION.

The series will continue to lend itself to the animated medium because of the protagonists' flights of fancy as they present over-the-top ways to tackle life's problems, some of which may actually try to be implemented with disastrous results as they tackle life's problems, integrating a level of humor not attained by the original show. Also, again as in the original show, ultimately a compromise comes about that must be real-world and yet innovative, at times a combination of several character's skills.

As a show geared to the audience that grew up on the original show, ANYTHING IS POSSIBLE: THE COLLEGE EDITION meets those viewers where they are at today just as they enter the college world. Tackling issues the viewers likely will encounter with a mix of over-the-top humor and serious overtones, the show channels the interest and energy the viewers spent in the original characters and mirrors their hopes and fears in the world of today. The ongoing theme of friendship to surviving life, carrying through from the original ANYTHING IS POSSIBLE series, will keep viewers coming back for more.

PROTAGONISTS

LYLIA – Lylia turned out to be beautiful but not a knockout like J.M., which continues to fuel a rivalry between the two women. In addition, Lylia now faces the most peer pressure of any of them as a pretty girl scientist. She experiments with physics, chemistry, biology, just to name some areas. Personality-wise she's open and outgoing and loves everyone. Her cousin is Rake, the visual artist. She shares a dorm room with Yazzmin, the new member of the cast.

Figure 3.2 – Page 1 of 3 of bible for *Anything is Possible: The College Edition*

RAKE - Who'd have thought it, the reclusive artist becoming a musclebound hunk? But that's exactly how things turned out for Rake. He took his frustrations and put them into weightlifting as that was physical education classes he could take and not have to participate in group things, a nd found he really liked it. Women want to flock to him because of his muscular build, but Rake's still got the mental walls of distance up around him unable to let anyone close. He also experiences great frustration because musclebound physique does not lend itself to the visual arts and just makes him more clumsy. Rake's into all forms of visual art, from painting to pottery and more. He shares a dorm room with Jonnie, much to his chagrin.

KAYLI – Kayli, no surprise, made it to college on an athletic scholarship. However, originally considered the prettiest of the bunch, Kayli went butch as her athletic career progressed and finds herself in somewhat of a sexuality identity crisis as she's exposed to new ideas up against the image of what an athlete is expected to be. Her dorm roommate assignment, much to her exasperation, is J.M.

MATT – Matt, the musician who started out seeming the most plain and insecure of the bunch, now sports a bit of a bad boy front and now isn't as close to his childhood friends, who still work on trying to renew friendships with him. An interesting plot point that unfolds over the early episodes is that J.M. and Matt dated in high school and even went to the Senior Prom together, but even more of a mystery than why they started dating is why they broke up. His dorm assignment has turned out to be his old friend Armano, with whom he's become even more distant since Armano left town during their high school years.

ARMANO – Armano's "in your face" attitude never quite left him, and he's become quite the gossip, though not necessarily intentionally, though he now is a loose-clothed, unshaven slacker in appearance. He still soaks up every detail around him quite well, and remains the most social and talkative of the bunch. He's transferred his talent of curiosity to the school newspaper and the on-air news program. If something's up at school, it will be hard to hide from "nosy news Armano," as many call him these days. An interesting point we learn early on is that Armano actually ended up attending high school out of the area and this is the first time in years he's seen his youthful friends. Armano shares a dorm room with Matt.

Figure 3.2 – Page 2 of 3 of bible for *Anything is Possible: The College Edition*

YAZZMIN - A new addition to the series, Yazzmin brings a different perspective. She had to earn every penny just to make it to college and continues to juggle work and school. Unlike the other characters who knew their paths earlier in life in the original series, Yazzmin's still the classic "undecided" freshman. Yazzmin will be torn as people try to influence her in different directions. Unlike the other main characters, Yazzmin's relationship with her family is very strained and she's very self-sufficient and remains very interested on the interaction between people, making her a strong candidate for psychology, education, or criminal justice. She's been paired in a dorm room with Lylia.

ANTAGONISTS
JONNIE - Compared to his twin sister J.M., Jonnie's overweight from too much junk food and time at the computer. His look screams "nerd," and he continues to be lazy on most things… except hacking computers and other things of similar interests. He loves surfing the net about girls, especially ones who would never dare to date him… or that he'd have the nerve to ask out. He shares a dorm room with Rake.

J.M. - Still full of attitude, J.M.'s turned out to be a buxom beauty in sharp contrast with her personality. All the guys in the cast (except Jonnie, who's ashamed to have her as a sister) find themselves conflicted as they have to admit she's attractive despite their past history. J.M. is involved in sorority events and all over the college social scene. She continues to hide her writing interest in fear of being seen as "nerdy." An interesting plot point that unfolds over the early episodes is that J.M. and Matt dated in high school and even went to the Senior Prom together, but even more of a mystery than why they started dating is why they broke up. To her extreme aggravation, J.M. ended up dorm partners with Kayli.

Figure 3.2 – Page 3 of 3 of bible for *Anything is Possible: The College Edition*

Springboard, Logline, and Premise

With guidelines in hand detailing the cast of characters, major locations, and rules of the world, now the individual tales that make up the ongoing story of this world need to be created. There are several approaches to doing this.

Springboard or Logline: Springboards and loglines both are very short statements of a story idea. Springboard occurs as a generic term for anything from which an idea can be launched, such as a single sentence (or less), or even a conceptual art drawing. The definition of a logline, however, is more specific and implies a tighter kernel of a more fleshed out idea; in two to three sentences, the beginning, middle, and end of a particular story concept are conveyed. Springboards or loglines tend to be generated by producers—largely dependent on personal preference of style—and then assigned out to writers to then be fleshed out into more detailed stories. Not all series have producers generating all series ideas; some series may have producers only handing out crucial ones for the season in this manner and then allowing pitches (suggestions by writers) for the remainder, but series where the overall series plotline is tightly controlled and therefore the producer needs to be more involved in the story process. However, for a variety of reasons that will be explored in Chapter 4, "Financing, Scheduling and Budgeting," such tightly controlled series are rare. Examples of shows with strong overall series plotlines, or "story arcs," are *Roughnecks: Starship Troopers Chronicles* (Sony), *Gargoyles* (Disney), and many of the action-adventure anime series that have been dubbed for foreign audiences such as the *YuGiOh!* franchise (NAS/TV TOKYO—English dub by 4Kids Entertainment). In prime-time animation, where a writers' roundtable approach is used, springboards and loglines are also more likely to be assigned. For animated feature films, springboards and loglines, except perhaps in an in-house company pitch situation or a case where the producer has the essence of the film idea but needs to hire someone for development, do not generally get used.

Premise: These will either be what writers create from springboards or loglines provided by the producer, or will submit directly to the producer based on their own thoughts after reading the series bible if independent pitches of episode ideas are taken. In the case of feature films, a premise might be implemented if the producer wants to get a general idea of where a writer wants to take his notion of a film without getting too in-depth, perhaps because the producer has not worked with the writer before and wants to get a feel of how the writer thinks without committing too much upfront. It gives a sense of beginning, middle, and end, with crucial plot turns and twists without too much detail.

Bear in mind that two plot threads at minimum exist, which are usually called the "A" story and the "B" story. The "A" story, or primary story, tends to be more action oriented as the characters try to reach the story goal; the "B" story focuses more on character growth and development. The two occur parallel to one another and usually come together by the end of the story.

What follows is a premise I wrote up for myself as I worked out a sample script based on my series bible for *Anything is Possible*. Like the bible, this sample episode was written several years before this book. I've left mostly everything just as I did it back then, errors and changes in thoughts included, to give a sense of how the documents themselves can evolve in the production process. The only exception is that the original script needed to be a 7-minute script for some reason I've long since forgotten, and since 11-minute and 22-minute scripts are the norm in series television (though a few series do 7-minute ones still), I did add a couple scenes which I feel enrich the story to the script to make it closer to the length for an 11-minute episode. The premise for the episode "Talent Show" follows as Figure 3.3.

Throughout this section, I will also present alternate examples using the *Anything is Possible: The College Edition* as my model. *Anything is Possible: The College Edition* was conceived as a 22-minute script concept, so only excerpts will be presented. I have included a premise for the episode "Freshman Orientation" as Figure 3.4 to show that not much difference exists at this stage between an 11-minute and 22-minute storyline.

<u>**ANYTHING IS POSSIBLE**</u>

"Talent Show"

Lylia, Rake, Armano, and Kayli help their friend Matt, who's afraid to enter the Talent Show. They provide creative ideas and a cool stage name but that's not the problem. After seeing school bullies J.M. and Jonnie give Matt a hard time, Lylia talks to Matt and finds he's afraid of people laughing at his music. Together, she and the other friends brainstorm ways to ignore what others think and Matt decides to write a funny song. At the show, J.M. goes on stage and recites bad poetry and the kids figure out she intimidated Matt so she didn't have to compete with Matt's poetic lyrics. Matt's a good sport to J.M. after she's laughed at, and everyone enjoys his song.

Figure 3.3 – Premise for *Anything is Possible* episode

ANYTHING IS POSSIBLE: THE COLLEGE EDITION

"Freshman Orientation"

A common college rite of passage provides the backdrop to
reunite the cast of the original series. Lylia, Rake and
Kayli show up and are surprised by their friend Armano who
left the high school years and just barely managed a last
minute enrollment transfer. They meet up with the rest of
their orientation group and find it includes not only a
very buxom J.M. who turns all the guys' heads and her
brother Jonnie who's not changed one bit aside from aging,
but their former friend Matt now gone distant rebel-boy.
Armano, who used to be close to Matt, wants to try to renew
the friendship but Matt brushes him off. This sets off
Armano's curiosity and he embarks on a quest to learn what
drove Matt away from the others, at times going to
hilarious lengths. Lylia, Rake, and Kayli -- still being
the true friends they are – follow Armano along to keep him
out of trouble, since they learned long ago there's no
stopping him. In the end, Armano has to come face to face
with the surprising truth that Matt and J.M. dated and went
to the senior prom, though they don't go together now and
that reason is another mystery for another time. The
episode ends with the characters getting their dorm
assignments, and Lylia getting a dorm mate she doesn't
recognize named Yazzmin… yet another mystery for another
time.

Figure 3.4 – Premise for *Anything is Possible: The College Edition* episode

Gardner's Guide to Writing and Producing Animation

Outline or Treatment

Once a premise gets approval, it needs to be fleshed out step by step and all scenes accounted for. Not only is this to firm up the story, but it gives the production team a heads up on how many characters, backgrounds, and props need to be created for the episode or film. Also, if for some reason the amount of items called for in the story exceeds what the budget can handle (if known yet, it probably will be if one has found the financiers at earlier stages versus writing the script on speculation to get the financiers; see Chapter 4, "Financing, Scheduling and Budgeting" for more information), those issues can be taken care of at this stage.

Generally, stories must be paced around a three-act structure, whether a television piece or feature film. This does not necessarily mean the animated project has that many commercial breaks (though it is true of a 22-minute episode); it refers to plot points and pacing. In fact, if one is writing a primetime animated comedy, it is very important to note the three act rule applies here versus the two acts of live-action television sitcoms. Two approaches exist to sketching out a story in a scene by scene manner.

Beat Outline: The beat outline breaks out the entire episode scene by scene. While it uses scene headings similar to the script, each scene then is described below it in a paragraph form, getting the crucial moments of each scene. First appearances of characters and major props are capitalized. An example of a beat outline for the *Anything is Possible* episode "Talent Show" appears as Figure 3.5. Note already a few slight differences from the premise. The specific focus of brainstorming a funny song with Matt no longer appears; in the outline he's more hung up with having a good image and stage name. The main reason for that ultimately came as from awareness on my part as I developed the story of the additional costs that would go into writing music if it was produced, and then all the rights issues connected with the music, so I dropped this as the reason the friends helped Matt (something that could very well happen with any producer developing an idea, so it makes a good real world example). Also, Matt almost seems to gloat over J.M.'s problems on stage instead of being the good sport that the premise pitched, which I would argue doesn't make him a good protagonist (and I did catch this in going to script, pay attention to how the story changes when we get to the script sample). Bear in mind this is the outline for the original 7-minute script which actually appears in an expanded 11-minute form in this book. I will comment more when we get to that step in the process.

Treatment: A treatment writes out the plotline of the animated project in a short story format, usually utilizing a paragraph per scene but the one paragraph rule is not hard and fast. There are no scene headings breaking things up, so judging a total number of locations is a bit more difficult to discern. First time appearances by characters are capitalized, as are major props. For a treatment example, see Figure 3.6, which features the first page of the treatment for the *Anything is Possible: The College Edition* episode, "Freshman Orientation."

ANYANG IS POSSIBLE
"Talent Show"
Outline by SHANNON MUIR

INT. SCHOOL - MAIN HALLWAY - DAY
LYLIA, RAKE, KAYLI, ARMANO, and MATT gather around poster
for talent show signup get egged by the J.M. and her
brother JONNIE. Matt has the hardest time signing and
won't do it. Why? He doesn't want to just be billed as
Matt, or so he says that's the only reason.

INT. LYLIA'S PARENT'S GARAGE - DAY
Others practice what they're going to do. Matt's not. He
says he's not interested. Why? He just can't come up with
a good stage name. The kids tap into their flights of
fancy to try to help him but it doesn't help, he just walks
off. The kids try to figure out how to find out what's
really up with Matt and what they should do to find out.

INT. SCHOOL - MAIN HALLWAY - DAY
School hallway, Matt encounters J.M. and Jonnie on his own
who try putting him down. The others hear this and tell
them "wait until you hear his Talent Show tune". J.M. and
Jonnie leave and Matt's mad at his friends, reminding them
"I told you I'm not doing that". They hit the nail on the
head by his response, telling him "you're afraid people
won't like your song". They remind him it's not about
making other people happy. But if everyone doesn't like
it, protests Matt, that's everyone in school. Someone
points out that if he doesn't perform now he'll never hear
the end of it from J.M. and Jonnie. He gulps, OK.

INT. SCHOOL AUDITORIUM - NIGHT
At the show, J.M. and Jonnie goad him that his music sucks
and everyone will just all laugh at him. It almost looks
they've won.

But in come the friends true to the end, and Matt bolstered
by the fact that J.M. has difficulty reciting her own,
personal, not-so-perfect poetry.

Matt ends it with going out there but his parting words are
"still got to think of a good stage name, for the day I
really break it big" and we intercut closeups of him
performing with the kids listening.

Figure 3.5 – Outline for *Anything is Possible* episode

ANYTHING IS POSSIBLE: THE COLLEGE EDITION
"Freshman Orientation"
Treatment by SHANNON MUIR

The episode opens at RAKE's parents' house. He's lounging on the couch as LYLIA puts all her energy into packing her bag. There's the sound of a car door pulling in and the energetic ring of the doorbell as Lylia answers the door to find KAYLI on the other side. Kayli's come to pick the two cousins up to carpool with them to freshman orientation. While his outer body may be handsome and muscular, Rake's never lost his dour personality and comes to odds with Kayli's bubby personality. Lylia steps in to try and cool things between them. Kayli goes for a playful jab at Rake just like old times, but his unforgiving muscle reminds her that there are some things she will still have to get used to.

Lylia, Rake, and Kayli pull up outside campus to attend freshman orientation. As Kayli struggles to get a parking space against maddening traffic, Rake mentions how it seems odd that Matt and Armano aren't there with them. Just then, someone pulls into a space Kayli was trying for and Rake starts screaming at the driver as Kayli and Lylia try to get him to shut up. The driver comes up to the side of the car and we find out it is… ARMANO! Quickly we pick up that he moved away for high school and because his life was so crazy he ended up having to compete for late admission and didn't even know if he'd make it. He looks around and asks about MATT, but everyone says that in high school he stopped hanging out with us, at least you would send email from far away. The happy reunion is rudely interrupted by students in their cars trapped behind Kayli, upset that she's stopped traffic. Armano promises to catch up with them inside.

Inside, Lylia, Rake and Kayli find Armano staring at a beautiful knockout of a girl who has guys literally drooling all about her. Armano asks if any of them happen to know who this lovely vision is, and Lylia tells him it's J.M. herself, their elementary school rival Juliet Meghan. This lets the wind out of Armano's sails as he never got along with J.M. He remarks that if anyone told him back then J.M. would turn out looking that way, he would have never believed it. Rake cracks back that they were all in 6th grade, the idea of any of us turning into what we have we'd never have believed. Armano wonders if J.M.'s brother JONNIE changed, and that question is answered as he comes in on the scene as a larger bumbling klutz version of his old self and embarrasses his twin sister.

Just then, the call goes out for everyone to enter the auditorium for orientation. Armano looks around desperately; Lylia asks who he's looking for. Armano confides he'd been holding out hope Matt would be here, he missed his old friend so much when he was away for high school. Lylia tries to gently warn Armano that maybe he should be grateful, because the Matt that graduated high school is not the Matt you last knew. Armano comments back then that they did know more than they were letting on in the parking lot. Kayli in her caring way underscores that they just don't want Armano getting hurt.

Figure 3.6 – First page of treatment for *Anything is Possible: The College Edition* episode

Script

As was said earlier in the chapter, live-action and animation scripts share many similarities; some in 3-D CGI may look exactly like live-action scripts. Both use similar means to indicate location, dialogue, and transitions that indicate a short or long passage of time. The most significant difference comes in the traditional animation format, where every shot is "called out," or described, including what characters are in each shot and the placement of the camera in relation to them. Bear in mind that these shot calls made by the writer can be overruled by the episodic director or the producer, yet unless something turns out to be in strong need of being reworked usually this does not happen due to time constraints.

Script becomes difficult to explain without illustration. Figure 3.7 shows a script for an 11-minute *Anything is Possible* version of "Talent Show" (though as we will learn later in the chapter, script length can be somewhat arbitrary), though the outline was for the 7-minute version. For the original 7-minute script, the outline in Figure 3.5 came pretty close to what I actually did in terms of number of scenes. However, as I said before, it was way too short for an 11-minute script, which is more commonplace which is why I expanded the final script to serve the readers as a better example. With what is shown in Figure 3.5 still being the major beats of the script in this chapter, pay attention to what got added in order to expand the script and how it helps plot and character. Also, note that Matt has gone back to being the more sympathetic self as pitched in the premise, though the concept of the funny song remained out of the script for reasons previously explained.

```
              ANYTHING IS POSSIBLE
                "Talent Show"
               by SHANNON MUIR

FADE IN:

INT. MIDDLE SCHOOL - HALLWAY - DAY
KAYLI, RAKE, LYLIA, MATT, and ARMANO gather around a TABLE.
A SIGNUP SHEET is on the table, with a PEN next to it, and
above the table hangs a BANNER that reads "Talent Show
Signup."

                    LYLIA
          Cool, a talent show!

LYLIA, RAKE, ARMANO - Lylia excitedly points at the banner.

                    LYLIA (cont'd)
          Maybe I could create a magic act with
          illusions based on scientific principles.

                    RAKE
          Boring.

                    ARMANO
               (sarcastic)
          Yo, like what are you going to do, Mr.
          Artiste?

                    RAKE
          Speed painting.  Faster than that guy on
          public teevee.

KAYLI, MATT - As Kayli signs the sheet.

                    KAYLI
          I'm going to do an aerobic dance routine.
               (to Matt)
          You going to perform, Matt?

                    MATT
          No, I don't think so.

OTS KAYLI - She looks over at Matt.

                    KAYLI
          Why not?  You write good songs.  Maybe I
          could dance to one of them.

Matt shrinks back.

                    MATT
          You're better off solo.
```

Figure 3.7 – Page 1 of 11 of script for *Anything is Possible*

GARDNER's Guide to Writing and Producing Animation

WIDE SHOT - Of the group.

              LYLIA
      Come on, if my stuck-up cousin Rake will
      get up on stage you can too. It'll be
      fun.

              RAKE
      Who you calling stuck-up?

              JONNIE (O.S.)
      If the shoe fits.

All heads turn as the camera PULLS BACK to reveal JONNIE and
his sister J.M. who approach Matt.

              J.M.
      Matt just can't hack getting up in front
      of people. He's a chicken.

J.M., MATT - Matt shakes nervously.

              MATT
      That's not true.

J.M. gestures toward the sign-up sheet.

              J.M.
      OK then sign up.

              MATT
      Well. Um.

LYLIA, RAKE, ARMANO, KAYLI - They move in to form a human
wall in front of Matt to shield him from J.M.

              LYLIA
      Leave him alone, J.M.!

              RAKE
      Don't see either of you stepping forward.

              ARMANO
      Hey, do you even have any talents other
      than bullying?

              KAYLI
      You could try being a little kinder.

JONNIE, J.M. - Jonnie steps forward.

              JONNIE
      We got lots of talent. I can win "Karma
      Challenge Eight" blindfolded!

Figure 3.7 – Page 2 of 11 of script for *Anything is Possible*

J.M. holds her hand up toward her little brother.

> J.M.
> Glad you're proud of your video game
> prowess, brother, but I don't think
> people can sit and watch you play that
> game for hours.

TRACK WITH J.M. over to the signup sheet, much to the
surprise of the other kids. She signs in.

> J.M. (cont'd)
> You'll see me there.

> ARMANO (O.S.)
> What are you going to do, be a standup
> comedian?

ANOTHER ANGLE - as J.M. turns to face the protagonists.

> J.M.
> Funny. Show up and see.

J.M. EXITS FRAME. As she does:

> J.M. (cont'd)
> If you're not chicken.

> DISSOLVE TO:

INT. LYLIA'S FAMILY'S HOUSE - GARAGE - DAY
The gang gathers in the garage at Lylia's family's house.

> KAYLI
> Don't let them get to you.

LYLIA, MATT - Everyone continues to encourage him.

> LYLIA
> Kayli's right. You can do it!

> MATT
> I need some kind of stage name. I can't
> be just plain old Matt.

> LYLIA
> I've got an idea.

LYLIA - TILT UP AS A THOUGHT BUBBLE showing an ELVIS-LIKE
MATT with a guitar forms over her head, then fills the
screen.

Figure 3.7 – Page 3 of 11 of script for *Anything is Possible*

EXT. CONCERT STAGE - DAY
Elvis-like Matt starts <PLAYING A 50s ROCK STYLE TUNE>.

> CHEERING CROWD (B-TRACK)
> <walla>

Over this:

> LYLIA (O.S.)
> How about Showstopper Matt?

ANOTHER ANGLE - Elvis-like Matt STOPS PLAYING, looks around
confused as:

> RAKE (O.S.)
> No no no!

With a magic POOF!, Elvis-like Matt becomes BEATNIK MATT.
Beatnik Matt <STARTS PLAYING A FOLKSY TUNE>.

> RAKE (cont'd)
> Matt the Talespinner.

CLOSE ON MATT - his face changes from the beatnik look to a
long-haired GOTH-MATT and his <GUITAR PLAYING BECOMES MORE
MODERN ROCK>.

> ARMANO
> I'm all for Dark Dude.

PULL BACK as Matt changes yet again, this Matte to COWBOY-
MATT and a <COUNTRY-WESTERN TUNE>.

> KAYLI
> How about Down-Home Matt?

INT. LYLIA'S FAMILY'S HOUSE - GARAGE - DAY
KAYLI, MATT, LYLIA - Matt shakes his head "no."

> MATT
> Thanks for trying.

OTS KAYLI - as Matt exits the garage.

> MATT (cont'd)
> It's probably best I don't perform.

LYLIA, KAYLI - Each look at the other, worried about their
friend.

> KAYLI
> Peer pressure's wrong. If he doesn't
> want to do it, we shouldn't make him.

Figure 3.7 – Page 4 of 11 of script for *Anything is Possible*

                          LYLIA
                Did Matt ever say he didn't want to be in
                the talent show?

                          KAYLI
                No.

        ARMANO, RAKE - Rake crosses his arms.

                          KAYLI (cont'd)
                He's so good. I don't understand.

                          RAKE
                So you think there's something secret
                reason he's not doing it? That's silly.

                          ARMANO
                We just got to ask Matt flat-out.

        CLOSE ON LYLIA

                          LYLIA
                Tomorrow at school, that's what we'll do.

INT. MIDDLE SCHOOL - HALLWAY - DAY
Matt walks down the hall past the talent show signup sheet.

                          LYLIA (V.O.)
                If he says he doesn't want to do it,
                we'll go with that.

        FOLLOW MATT as he goes over and looks at it.

                          J.M. (O.S.)
                Still don't see your name, chicken.

        OTS MATT - of J.M.

                          MATT
                I still could.

                          J.M.
                Then do it now.

        MATT - hand shaking, slowly picks up the pen on the table.
        As he goes to sign his name:

                          LYLIA (O.S.)
                Matt, wait!

        LYLIA, MATT, J.M. - Lylia comes down the hall.

Figure 3.7 – Page 5 of 11 of script for *Anything is Possible*

> LYLIA (cont'd)
> If you don't want to perform just say so.

> MATT
> It's just that--

Lylia looks over at Matt.

> LYLIA
> (to J.M.)
> Get lost.

J.M. - points to herself.

> J.M.
> I'm going to win anyway, so why bother?

J.M. EXITS FRAME.

MATT, LYLIA - Lylia reaches out to grab hold of the pen.
They both hold on to it.

> LYLIA
> Matt, you don't sign up but you don't say
> no. I'll take the pen, you don't have to
> feel pressured.

> MATT
> But I really do want to be part of the
> talent show.

> LYLIA
> Then why not sign up?

LYLIA - looks at her friend concerned.

> LYLIA (cont'd)
> Are you afraid people won't like your
> song?

OTS LYLIA - Matt lets go of the pen and puts his hands in his
pockets.

> LYLIA (cont'd)
> Is that why you back off when J.M. calls
> you chicken?

> MATT
> Yeah. I have nightmares of everyone
> laughing at me.

Lylia TURNS TO FACE CAMERA and motions Matt to walk with her
down the hall.

Figure 3.7 – Page 6 of 11 of script for *Anything is Possible*

                         LYLIA
                    Let's go have lunch.

                                              DISSOLVE TO:

INT. MIDDLE SCHOOL - CAFETERIA - DAY
Lylia, Matt, Rake, Kayli, and Armano eat LUNCH together.

                         RAKE
                    Just get over it.

RAKE, KAYLI - Kayli gives Rake a playful jab in the ribs.

                         KAYLI
                    Come on, Rake, you're not helping to
                    encourage him.

                         RAKE
                    Yes I am. I don't worry about what
                    others think.

ARMANO - He speaks up to offer a constructive suggestion.

                         ARMANO
                    It's like how I deal with doing oral
                    reports in class.

TILT UP AS A THOUGHT BUBBLE showing an STATELY DRESSED ARMANO
delivering a speech, holding papers in his hand, surrounded
by 6th graders DRESSED AS REPORTERS.

                         ARMANO (cont'd) (V.O.)
                    I pretend I'm an important press
                    secretary addressing the media.

                                              MATCH DISSOLVE TO:

THOUGHT BUBBLE WITH KAYLI - Now it is Kayli standing at on a
podium in RUNNING CLOTHES, but it is waving to a crowd of
regularly dressed 6th grade students holding FLOWERS and with
some kind of GOLD MEDAL around her neck like an Olympic or
similar athlete.

                         KAYLI (V.O.)
                    I always imagine I've won the greatest
                    race of my life.

                                              MATCH DISSOLVE TO:

Figure 3.7 – Page 7 of 11 of script for *Anything is Possible*

THOUGHT BUBBLE WITH LYLIA - When Lylia is shown giving the
report, she's in A LAB COAT speaking to other 6th grade
SIMILARLY CLOTHES SCIENTISTS as she demonstrates a chemistry
experiment with two beakers.

> LYLIA (V.O.)
> And I think of it as the most important
> science breakthrough of my career that
> I'm ready to share with the world.

As Lylia pours the liquid from one beaker to the other, SMOKE
is created that totally engulfs the thought bubble as we
TILT DOWN to Lylia at the cafeteria table.

> LYLIA (cont'd)
> See, Matt, it all depends on how you
> decide to deal with it.

LYLIA, MATT - Matt's now far more eager.

> LYLIA (cont'd)
> Being scared is only a problem if you let
> it be.

> MATT
> You're right, Lylia. I'll sign up right
> now!

Matt jumps out of his seat and runs O.S., leaving his friends
smiling.

                                                    DISSOLVE TO:

INT. MIDDLE SCHOOL - AUDIOTORIUM - BACKSTAGE - EVENING
A 50s style song plays. Matt tunes his guitar, dressed just
in his normal clothes. Armano's also dressed normally. Lylia
wears a magic hat and cape. Rake's in a messy painting
smock.

ENTERS FRAME as she comes running back to meet her
friends, having just finished a dance routine. She's dressed
in a poodle skirt outfit.

> KAYLI
> That was fun! Matt, you'll like it too.
> It's a great crowd.

J.M. and Jonnie approach.

                         JONNIE
              Look, J.M., his friends pressured him to
              come.

                         MATT
              Did not! I came because I wanted to.

                         J.M.
              I'm still going to win.

Lylia cups a hand to her ear as if trying to listen.

                         LYLIA
              I think I just heard them call your name.
              "Juliet Meghan!"

                         J.M.
              That's J.M. to you!

J.M. takes a piece of paper out of her pocket and EXITS
FRAME.

INT. MIDDLE SCHOOL - AUDIOTORIUM - STAGE - EVENING
Under the lights, J.M. starts to read.

                         J.M.
              Colors are all around me, red and blue
              and even green,

INT. MIDDLE SCHOOL - AUDIOTORIUM - BACKSTAGE - EVENING

                         J.M. (B-TRACK)
              From these come other colors too, In the
              vibrant world of me and you.

                         ARMANO
              No wonder she didn't want Matt to
              compete. She's a poet!

                         KAYLI
              Poetry is a lot like music lyrics.

                         RAKE
              Pretty lousy poetry, if you ask me.

                         MATT
              Hey, at least she's trying. She'll
              probably get better with practice.

                         LYLIA
              You're defending her?

Figure 3.7 – Page 9 of 11 of script for *Anything is Possible*

                              MATT
                    She was insecure too. That's why she did
                    what she did. Maybe I didn't like how
                    she treated me, but I understand why now.

From the stage J.M. finishes her poetry. The crowd's
reaction is heard.

                              CROWD
                    <taunting giggles and laughter walla>

J.M. ENTERS FRAME, her poem crumpled and her head hung low.
Jonnie comes up to his sister.

                              MATT
                    Hey, J.M.?

OTS MATT - Of J.M. and Jonnie. J.M. looks at Matt.

                              MATT (cont'd)
                    Good effort.

J.M. turns and walks away. Jonnie follows.
MATT - adjusts his guitar.

                              MATT (cont'd)
                    I'm next.

WIDE SHOT - Matt EXITS FRAME to go on stage. After a beat,
we hear his <GUITAR> begin to play. His friends start
dancing to the music, even Rake.

                              LYLIA
                    Go Matt!

                              RAKE
                    I told him, don't worry about what others
                    think.

                              KAYLI
                    You're a winner no matter what!

                              ARMANO
                    Keep it up, my friend!

INT. MIDDLE SCHOOL - AUDIOTORIUM - STAGE - EVENING
Matt continues, totally into playing his guitar. He doesn't
play attention to anything else around him.

INT. MIDDLE SCHOOL - AUDIOTORIUM - BACKSTAGE - EVENING

His friends watch as they hear the crowd goes wild.

Figure 3.7 – Page 10 of 11 of script for *Anything is Possible*

ANYTHING IS POSSIBLE: "Talent Show" 11.

CROWD
<cheer walla>

Kayli jumps for joy, the others <APPLAUD>.

FADE OUT.

<u>THE END</u>

Figure 3.7 – Page 11 of 11 of script for *Anything is Possible*

In contrast, a prime-time animation script more closely resembles a live-action sitcom script. This is for several reasons. First of all, early modern prime-time animation writers (referring to *The Simpsons* and forward) came out of sketch comedy such as *The Tracey Ullman Show* or out of live-action sitcoms, as did many of the actors. Since they already had a familiarity with the double spaced dialogue that serves as the main difference between the two, it remained in the prime-time animation style as the standard to today. Also, the prime-time animation series tend to devote a budget for last minute ADR changes to be more topical on their first airing, so the double spaced dialogue allows for easy "on the fly" rewrites.

Outside of that, all other elements of the script conform to the more traditional and standard animation format. This includes scene headings, sound effects, parenthetical usage, and capitalization on first appearances, just to name a few things.

To compare with the complete script just presented, Figure 3.8 presents the opening scenes of the "Freshman Orientation" episode of *Anything is Possible: The College Edition.*

ANYING IS POSSIBLE: THE COLLEGE EDITION
"Freshman Orientation"
Written by
SHANNON MUIR

ACT ONE

FADE IN:

INT. RAKE'S FAMILY'S HOUSE - LIVING ROOM - DAY

RAKE flips through the channels on the television,
finding nothing of interest on. A packed gym-style
bag is near his feet.

In the background, his cousin carefully LYLIA
finishes packing materials into a backpack.

Rake yawns, but stops flipping channels when he
hears an <ENGINE> outside.

                    LYLIA

          Sounds like Kayli's here!

EXT. RAKE'S FAMILY'S HOUSE - DAY

KAYLI's car pulls up into the drive. Kayli comes
bounding out and up to the door.

INT. RAKE'S FAMILY'S HOUSE - DAY

The bell rings and Lylia throws open the door,
revealing an ectremely energetic Kayli.

                    KAYLI

          (SCREAMS) Who's up for rocking

          freshman orientation?

Rake slowly gets up off the couch and picks up his
bag, puts it over his arm.

                    RAKE

          Why do you treat this like we won the

          lottery or something? We got into

          college. So?

Figure 3.8 – Page of script for *Anything is Possible: The College Edition*

Kayli's energy lessens.

                        KAYLI

        Man, you still know how to rain on a

        parade, don't you, Rake? Would have

        thought all the girls giving you the

        eye from those pecs might have changed

        your demeanor.

Rake points over to Kayli.

                        RAKE

        Interesting comment from one who

        doesn't exactly have the guys lining

        up for her.

Lylia steps between the two of them, a smile on her
face but knowing this could go the wrong way any
second. She puts an arm around each one of her
friends.

                       LYLIA

        (CALMING DEMEANOR) Hey, hey, we're all

        friends here. And in the end that's

        what counts, right?

                        KAYLI

        Absolutely!

                        RAKE

        Just like old times, as much as we

        still can, anyway.

                        KAYLI

        See, there's hope for you yet!

Figure 3.8 – Page of script for *Anything is Possible: The College Edition*

```
Kayli tries to jab Rake in the ribs, but winces in
pain as she hits muscle.  She looks down puzzled at
her hand.

                    KAYLI (cont'd)

         That is still going to take some

         getting used to.
```

Figure 3.8 – Page of script for *Anything is Possible: The College Edition*

Gardner's Guide to Writing and Producing Animation

Storyboard

As stated earlier, the option does exist of telling the whole story straight to board without a script. This can be an especially effective choice if one has art abilities and are working on one's own short cartoon. As to how much detail a storyboard should contain in regard to its panel count, the content should be enough to capture all the key poses plus enough to properly space out under each panel of dialogue. It is best to take this into early consideration before reaching the animatic stage (see Chapter 7, "Pre-Production") so one does not have to be bogged down by as many timing issues later. Also by having a sense of pace on the page, the board becomes more of an enjoyable read for the non-artist. This is important because for a pitch, the audience generally consists of executives and other key contacts that may have creative backgrounds but not necessarily an art background. Also be aware that many shows that do script to storyboard (such as Cartoon Network shows like *Spongebob Squarepants* or *Camp Lazlo*) do at least progress to the outline stage and make sure that outline is firm before proceeding with visuals.

WHICH METHOD SHOULD A PRODUCER USE?

Ultimately, one should lean toward whatever technique best utilizes your talents to sell your idea. If someone's gift is words over art, a small "mini bible" for a pitch that boils down the essence of characters, location, and theme may be the best choice (though it can help to hire an artist in a style a producer feels matches his or her vision of the work to at least do some conceptual drawings). For the more art minded, it may be best to get the point across with a storyboard, albeit a short one that just gives a taste of the characters in their world.

STORY PLANNING

For an animated feature film—and for the sake of this discussion it is being assumed the producer is not making a sequel to an existing property—debate comes around whether or not "seeds for sequels" should be planted in a script. There have been a few cases where a company, desperate to gain more mileage from a hit animated film, has done things (such as the "prequel" billed as a sequel, or building them around popular sidekicks who can't hold their own film) that the original presentation may or may not have lent itself to. For the sake of the story, and the current animation climate of direct to DVD follow up films, it may be advisable to at least gauge where sequel potential is in the current story and make sure it holds up throughout. However, do not let the integrity of the current story suffer because of having sequels in mind.

In the case of a series, having episodes with a strong continuity that must be aired in a specific order does carry advantage. For one, it provides a natural hook to keep a viewer coming back for more of the story. Another, it helps the producer set out a clear overall map of the vision early on. However, some definite disadvantages also exist. The largest is if viewers miss early episodes and come in later, they may get lost and quickly lose interest (some shows counteract this by providing a recap of the prior episode, but this only helps to a point and is not a cure-all substitute). Even more challenging comes from the production end, in the form of unexpected production delays (more on this in Chapter Four, "Financing, Scheduling and Budgeting"). However, just as in the advice for feature film, make sure an episode holds its own. Each episode should have its own beginning, middle, and conclusion contributing to the larger arc with cliffhangers used sparingly. This way a first time or occasional viewer is more likely to be left satisfied versus frustrated. Remember that one of the goals is to have something to "leave behind" later after you try to pitch, or sell yourself, to executives (more on this in Chapter 4, "Financing, Scheduling and Budgeting"). To this end while an outline or full script may be helpful for a producer behind the scenes, they are not useful initially for pitching to others. However if people are interested and want to see more, a producer better be prepared!

IS THERE SUCH A THING AS A WRITER/PRODUCER?

This chapter spends a lot of time talking about the producer hiring and guiding someone through development, and only on a few occasions has hinted at the idea that a producer can also perform writing duties. To clarify, the concept of a Writer/Producer does exist in animation, though the concept did not get detailed exploration there since not all producers are writers, and Chapter 1 more focuses on the different shades of a producer title. In fact, a Writer/Producer usually is not credited this way at all, but simply by the appropriate producer title. Generally a Writer/Producer wears two hats: one for the creative aspects of the show, the other for managing the day-to-day workflow. Often this individual will have been the developer of the show and then continued to stay on through the process, but not always.

SPOTLIGHT INTERVIEW

GREG WEISMAN

Greg Weisman is an accomplished animation writer/producer who began his career as a writer for DC Comics before transitioning into animation. He produced the second season of *W.I.T.C.H.* but is best known for his extensive involvement creating and producing the *Gargoyles* animated series. In addition, Mr. Weisman has been an executive involved in the creation of animated television series for Disney and Dreamworks. He also has a background in voice direction, serving as voice director for Disney's DVD feature *Atlantis II: Milo's Return* and anime voice-dubbing for *New Generation Pictures*. Greg's extensive credits as a writer and story editor for animated series include *Kim Possible, The Batman, Roughnecks: The Starship Troopers Chronicles, Max Steel, Ben Ten,* as well as contributing to the animated feature *Bionicle – Mask of Light*. He shares some thoughts on what it means to have the title of producer on a show.

Now in terms of developing a show that likewise is different from series to series, I've been on shows where I developed a show from day one— *Gargoyles* is an example—and went on to be, uh, co-producer of the show initially, then producer of the show, then supervising producer of the show. All three of those titles I did the exact same job. I've been on other shows where I came in for example on the second season of *W.I.T.C.H.*, and from the point I started I had the exact same job producing the show and I wasn't involved in the development of the series because I was coming in on the second series. We had to do a little bit of re-development to sort of say, 'OK, how are we going to take this forward now?' because the first season of *W.I.T.C.H.* sort of ended the story and we had to sort of work out what we were going to do next. I wouldn't call that true development and there isn't any rule that a producer always is involved in the development, and often what you see happen is a producer or someone who could have been a producer develops a show and doesn't necessarily take it forward, or does but gets removed by a studio, or doesn't continue on to other seasons.

I'm clearly biased because as a writing producer and as a writer, I tend to want even in the visual medium that's animation to give the writer more authority. And that's not to say it isn't a collaborative medium but my personal experience is that the writer has to come up with these things from more or less thin air often if not always and I'd say seven times out of ten that means that the writer, or at least the writing producer, is the person with the vision to sort of carry through. I think it's amazing how little respect generally writers get in, in Hollywood in general but certainly in the animation business. Having said that, I mean the writing process—to step back for a second, it's just pretty basic, you know. If you've developed a good series, particularly one that's kind of humming, the characters sort of will tell you what happens next, but you come up with a springboard.

As a producer I often came up with all the springboards for my series; that is, one or two lines, I mean notions—sometimes sentences, sometimes ideas, sometimes visuals—that sort of, this is where the episode's gonna come out of and usually I would hand those off to my writers. Most of the show's that I've worked on as a producer, I've brought my writing team together not in sort of a sitcom sense where everyone is around the table contributing jokes to everybody else's script, but just I've got seven springboards here, let's bring seven writers in, we'll all talk about all seven, try to get a good arc going for those seven episodes, and then assign each of those seven writers a premise. They all might have contributed a little to the other story but at that point the seven sort of go off on their own. Since they're all freelancing in this day and age, we don't have that sort of luxury to have a full writer's table on every episode. And so the writers then go off, write premises, come back to me. I'll give notes, maybe put them to a second draft or maybe just rewrite it on my own.

I'm a very firm believer in really nailing an outline. I don't like to go to script with the story sort of vague in my head and figuring we'll solve a lot of problems at the script stage because that tends to cause more problems than it solves in my experience. So I'm a firm believer in outlines being very specific and detailed. I don't need to choreograph a whole battle scene in an outline, it's enough to say 'OK, they fight'—you know, I want all the story beats, beat by beat, in that outline, whether it's a beat outline or literally a full sort of treatment, I want it all spelled out, I want to make sure that the story's tracking before I send anyone to script. That way, the script stage becomes easy, or relatively easy, in that all you're sort of doing is taking this outline and fleshing it out with dialogue and a little more description, camera angles and stuff like that, but you're not trying to solve story problems at the script stage.

You should try as much as possible to think of animation as an assembly line, that you do each step and try and get each step as good as possible and then move on to the next step and not think of it as something where 'hey, I'm at script, I'm not sure I like the premise of this story' or 'I'm gonna change how this story breaks down'; in other words, trying to do the premise stage at the outline stage or the script stage tends to lead towards disaster. Now I say tends because there are exceptions. I've certainly been at work on plenty of scripts where I came up with a brilliant idea after the fact. But brilliant ideas should tend to make things easier. I'm not saying it isn't a lot of work to take a brilliant idea and run it through a script that's already existing, it is a lot of work, but it shouldn't be hard work. If it's truly a brilliant idea, the work should be easy; it could be substantial, but still easy. Brilliance should make things easier, not harder, and if you find yourself slogging through something because of a quote unquote 'brilliant idea' you came up with way after the stage where it should have come in, then the odds are it probably wasn't that brilliant to begin with. I'm sure there are plenty of exceptions to that as well. But I do think it behooves a producer, a story editor, and certainly a writer, to go in a step by step vein. Get an interesting springboard, get a premise that's got a good story to tell, get an outline that breaks that story down clearly, and then write a great script or as great as a script as you can.

The key thing for a producer is to make sure that all the building blocks are present in their development materials. Do we know what the basic concept for the series is? Do we know who each of the major characters are? Do we know at least a little bit about the minor characters? Do we know how the world operates, what the rules are? You know, do we know the major settings of this thing? Do we know the tone? Those things I think should all exist in the original development materials, and if you are a writing producer you should figure that stuff out. If you are not the writing producer, you should work with your writer, your story editor, to figure that stuff out so that when you hit the ground again in a step by step vein by the time you're sitting down trying to come up with springboards, trying to come up with premises, certainly long before you're writing scripts, that information is already part of the show's working parameters. It's not something you're figuring out as you go. Now, you know, sometimes time is a huge factor and I've seen shows, worked on shows where you had to work things out because you're given an assignment, you're given a schedule and you just didn't have time to get everything figured out in advance. But it, again, it behooves you to figure out as much of that stuff sooner than later, and try to work it out, try to nail it down."

"As a writer/producer, or rather as a producer who happens to also write, if I'm doing post production on a show and I see… here's a good example from *W.I.T.C.H.*, I had a character seeing a character for the first time in years and she says to her something along the lines of: 'The years have been good to you, I love the white hair.' We get the footage back. The woman she's talking to has blond hair. We're like going okay, let's cut the second half of the line. That's an edit, it's not as simple as saying cut the line, its already been animated, so we just cut away from the scene before she says the second half of the line so she just says 'The years have been good to you' instead of 'The years have been good to you, love the white hair.' One might argue, well call a retake so that the hair is white and that would be great if it were just in one scene, but if you realize that this character's appeared in this entire episode with blond hair then it's just not worth making those, that many changes for one line of dialogue though. Now I know there are a lot of shows these days, and I haven't actually worked on them as a producer—again, it's not the way I prefer to work—that uses a lot of

ADR and has an ADR budget and writing is done after the fact. And again, um, that's great but most of the shows I work on don't have an ADR budget, can't afford to do more dialogue after the fact, have to live either with the dialogue you have or to remove dialogue that you have.

I feel vaguely very partisan in the responses I've given so far in that they are all very from the point of view of the writer/producer and promoting his or her authority over the overall picture. And I don't mean to slight the great director/producers and art producers. It's not a cartoon without them. I can't draw anything but stick figures and so certainly I can't make a cartoon on my own, and any decent art directing /producer can make one without a writer. Can, without a doubt. One could argue how good it is, but at least they can do it, I can't. I don't mean to slight them, but I do think that I have just the tiniest bit of a chip on my shoulder, it's because I do think there's a tendency to, because animation is without a doubt a visual medium, to just run roughshod over writers, or not partner an art producer with a writing producer. I think that's a mistake, because I think that 9 times out of 10 what makes animation work is great story and great characters and most of that comes off the script page. Without that, I think you're really missing a piece and it's an important piece."

SUMMING IT ALL UP

Producers should care about writing because there is nothing to produce without a story. Many software programs exist on the market to help with get the script into a proper format. How much material should be made in advance for investors depends upon a producer's personal credibility in the business, a producer's strengths and weaknesses, and the business needs of the potential business partner or financier. A producer can either do development and writing his or herself or hire a writer with expertise to put together the series bible. Steps for the evolution of a story to be ready to go into pre-production include a premise, an outline or treatment, and a script. An alternate story design approach for a producer with art skills is a storyboard with dialogue. Stories in television can be planned to be either self-contained episodes, or part of a larger story arc, though some specific additional issues must be taken into consideration for those series that depend on an airing order.

CHAPTER FOUR

Financing, Scheduling, and Budgeting

THE THREE OFTEN FORGOTTEN STEPS

With a clearly thought out idea in hand, it would seem that a producer would be ready to start making his or her dream project. However, there are three items often overlooked until the last possible moment. These areas are financing, scheduling, and budgeting. The following chapter looks at how to approach these three areas, without which full scale production cannot commence.

WHO IS THE AUDIENCE?

Before a producer can consider financing, the primary audience needs determined. This is not to say that the movie or series cannot end up having something to offer a wide variety of people; in fact, those added side benefits are all to the better. Potential investors for financing, however, will want to know what the "target audience" the producer has in mind for the project. After all, the financiers have their own goals and objectives that rotate around reaching a select group of people, and need to make sure the two visions (the producer's and their own) will be in sync with one another.

Also, financiers tend to find comfort in things not being too radical a departure from what is known to succeed. Hence the classic mention of people looking for something like a current smash hit, "only different" so as not to be seen as a ripoff. So, in order to make this comparison, a producer must get a handle on what currently is on the market that is comparable to the product he or she wants to make, and find out the similarities and differences. If material exists with similar subject matter but targets a different age group (like the difference between the two *Anything is Possible* pitches), the producer can explain how a currently underserved audience can be reached by a hit show that is similar to something else yet has just enough twists for the other audience to appreciate. Sometimes the comparisons aren't as clear cut as that, however, and comparisons hinge on things as thin as similarities in the cast of character personalities but totally different storylines. The trick is putting a positive spin on anything that might make this idea interesting to someone else.

That said, a producer should not put too much emphasis on how "marketable" the concept is for toys, videogames, or any other tie-ins. While these certainly could be seen as side benefits, what remains of utmost importance to any investor is why money should be put up behind the property now in this specific form. Otherwise, one could argue to market the item in another media first and then create the animated project based on that interest. That ultimately could be how the investor wants to see the project get funded based on connections the investing person or entity may have, but those should be choices suggested by the investor and not the producer.

PLACES TO FIND FINANCIERS AND BUSINESS PARTNERS

A producer might get lucky soliciting for financiers on the Internet, and many try, but this is a risky long shot. Instead of going to places where the odds of finding reputable individuals with actual assets to throw behind the production are greater, a producer risks exposure to all comers with less than noble intentions.

The key is to look for strengths. Some financiers can give backing in the form of direct funds. Other financiers and production co-partners come in the form of "in kind" services, where they bring their company to the table instead of the original producer struggling with worrying about outsourcing. A producer weighs what options would be best for the production, and stays open to them all.

So where should a producer look for financiers?

Festivals such as MIP, Annecy, and Cannes are some of the most likely places to find these individuals. They will likely be attending in regard to properties that they are already involved in. Remember, these are places one may ultimately want to exhibit at so it is good to find like-minded individuals in that environment.

However, bear in mind that many meetings may have already been scheduled before they arrive and how open they are with last-minute plans is a matter of personal taste. A producer may have to settle for a lot of quick introductions and exchanged business cards with follow-up later. This same rule of thumb holds true with industry networking seminars, usually ones focusing on business over creative issues. Networking is always part of the game, but people usually do also attend hoping to gain new insight or information.

When a producer does finally get a meeting, in most cases it will only be to present the idea in broad strokes. Always remember that before the meeting, a producer should find out as much as can be learned about the potential investor, not only to see if they are a reliable prospect but also to help steer the conversation and build a common ground with the person or persons. A copy of the mini-bible or similar document becomes a "leave behind" for the potential investor to review after the meeting to consider the decision.

CREATIVE COMPROMISES WITH BUSINESS PARTNERS

One of the challenges of trying to get others to come on board to produce an animated concept is that they all want their "little stamp" on the creative property. The financiers tend to, in varying degrees, say variants of "I'm willing to come on board if…" certain conditions are met. Sometimes, as more partners come on board, these requests come in conflict with one another, resulting in a challenging balancing act. Sometimes the conditions are cultural. A financier may be well aware that a show will not play in their home country because certain content will offend or be misinterpreted (such as hand gestures, which are why many animated series avoid the use of them). Others are just simply the personal preferences of the financier. So no matter how trivial a request from a financier may seem, treat all these notes with equal weight and carefully examine why such a note is being made, to determine which ones can be negotiated and which ones clearly will be a deal-breaker if one pursues trying to amend them.

SETTING THE SCHEDULE PACE

The first thing to determine is the delivery date, regardless of whether film or television is being discussed. Everything works backwards from the delivery date accordingly. The major question is how much time to allow for each step in the production. A producer must remain aware that some areas will overlap (such as music from pre-production onwards, or major models being created at a story's outline stage).

There are a few rules of thumb that are fairly consistent. For example, in my experience in television animation, two weeks were almost always allotted for rough boards for a 22-minute episode and two weeks for clean-up; therefore, about a week apiece should be able to be allotted for an 11-minute board or less. Having said that, many factors become dictated by the reality of other people's schedules that must be accommodated (such as voice actors for recordings), whether or not work must be split between one or multiple animation studios, availability at the post house, etc. Therefore, it becomes difficult to suggest any hard and fast rules for a given situation. Also, each type of animation (2D, 3D, Flash) takes a different amount of time to complete, dependent not only by the nature of the type but by the capability of the crew that gets assigned to work on it. An animation house could have 'A', 'B', and 'C' level teams and the price being paid for the work or schedule delays leave a producer with the 'C' level team whose lesser quality and higher error rate cost a producer more time and retakes. Ultimately, with any of these three areas, it all comes back to the emphasis of Chapter 1 and the qualities of an effective producer. A producer should know the areas where he or she needs additional support. This producer then identifies those with strong skills who will help make the production stronger by becoming part of the essential team. There will be introductions to the major players of the animation staff in Chapter 6, "Meet the Players."

Numbering systems vary by studio. Also, once production is underway, some productions add another line under each set of due dates reflecting when items actually are submitted, to see how far off original estimates they end up being. producers track all pre- and post-production steps in detail and time at the animation house as a general number of weeks. A sample schedule for a season of an animated series (in this case, a proposed production schedule for a 6 episode run of *Anything is Possible* assuming a 2D animation style, had it ever become a series) appears on the next three pages as Figure 4.1. Note how, since each 22-minute episode would consist of two 11-minute pieces, how the production schedule needs to be laid out; "production number" refers to the number each script tracks by, while "episode number" indicates the number assigned to the finished show.

ANYTHING IS POSSIBLE
Season 1
PROJECTED SCHEDULE

Episode	Production Number	Episode Number	Premise Due	Outline Due	First Draft Script Due	Final Draft Script Due	Record Date	Preliminary Designs Due	Rough Storyboard Due	Final Storyboard Due
"First Day"	101A	101	8/14/06	8/21/06	9/5/06	9/11/06	9/18/06	9/18/06	9/25/06	10/2/06
"Talent Show"	101B	101	8/14/06	8/21/06	9/5/06	9/11/06	9/18/06	9/18/06	9/25/06	10/2/06
"Treasures"	102A	102	8/21/06	8/28/06	9/11/06	9/18/06	9/25/06	9/25/06	10/2/06	10/9/06
"I Wish I Was…"	102B	102	8/21/06	8/28/06	9/11/06	9/18/06	9/25/06	9/25/06	10/2/06	10/9/06
"Honor"	103A	103	8/28/06	9/5/06	9/18/06	9/25/06	10/2/06	10/2/06	10/9/06	10/16/06
"Daydreamer's Nightmare"	103B	103	8/28/06	9/5/06	9/18/06	9/25/06	10/2/06	10/2/06	10/9/06	10/16/06
"Give & Take"	104A	104	9/5/06	9/11/06	9/25/06	10/2/06	10/9/06	10/9/06	10/16/06	10/23/06
"I Dare You"	104B	104	9/5/06	9/11/06	9/25/06	10/2/06	10/9/06	10/9/06	10/16/06	10/23/06
"Busted!"	105A	105	9/11/06	9/18/06	10/2/06	10/9/06	10/16/06	10/16/06	10/23/06	10/30/06
"All's Fair…"	105B	105	9/11/06	9/18/06	10/2/06	10/9/06	10/16/06	10/16/06	10/23/06	10/30/06
"Perspectives" – Part 1	106A	106	9/18/06	9/25/06	10/9/06	10/16/06	10/23/06	10/23/06	10/30/06	11/6/06
"Perspectives" – Part 2	106B	106	9/18/06	9/25/06	10/9/06	10/16/06	10/23/06	10/23/06	10/30/06	11/6/06

Figure 4.1 – Production schedule 1 of 3

ANYTHING IS POSSIBLE
Season 1
PROJECTED SCHEDULE

Episode	Production Number	Episode Number	Rough Animatic Due	Final Animatic Due	Sheet Timing Due	Lip Sync Due	Final Models Due	Checking Due	Ship Date	Color Due	Color Ship Date
"First Day"	101A	101	10/9/06	10/16/06	10/23/06	10/25/06	10/25/06	10/27/06	10/30/06	11/6/06	11/13/06
"Talent Show"	101B	101	10/9/06	10/16/06	10/23/06	10/25/06	10/25/06	10/27/06	10/30/06	11/6/06	11/13/06
"Treasures"	102A	102	10/16/06	10/23/06	10/30/06	10/31/06	10/31/06	11/1/06	11/6/06	11/13/06	11/20/06
"I Wish I Was…"	102B	102	10/16/06	10/23/06	10/30/06	10/31/06	10/31/06	11/1/06	11/6/06	11/13/06	11/20/06
"Honor"	103A	103	10/23/06	10/30/06	11/6/06	11/8/06	11/8/06	11/10/06	11/13/06	11/20/06	11/27/06
"Daydreamer's Nightmare"	103B	103	10/23/06	10/30/06	11/6/06	11/8/06	11/8/06	11/10/06	11/13/06	11/20/06	11/27/06
"Give & Take"	104A	104	10/30/06	11/6/06	11/13/06	11/15/06	11/15/06	11/17/06	11/20/06	11/27/06	12/4/06
"I Dare You"	104B	104	10/30/06	11/6/06	11/13/06	11/15/06	11/15/06	11/17/06	11/20/06	11/27/06	12/4/06
"Busted!"	105A	105	11/6/06	11/13/06	11/20/06	11/22/06	11/22/06	11/27/06	11/27/06	12/4/06	12/11/06
"All's Fair…"	105B	105	11/6/06	11/13/06	11/20/06	11/22/06	11/22/06	11/27/06	11/27/06	12/4/06	12/11/06
"Perspectives" – Part 1	106A	106	11/13/06	11/20/06	11/27/06	11/29/06	11/29/06	12/1/06	12/4/06	12/11/06	12/18/06
"Perspectives" – Part 2	106B	106	11/13/06	11/20/06	11/27/06	11/29/06	11/29/06	12/1/06	12/4/06	12/11/06	12/18/06

Figure 4.1 – Production schedule 2 of 3

ANYTHING IS POSSIBLE
Season 1
PROJECTED SCHEDULE

Episode	Production Number	Episode Number	Footage Delivered	Rough Music Due	Work Print and Color Correction	Rough Video & Audio Due	Final Mix	Locked Picture Due	Closed Captioning Due	Delivery Date
"First Day"	101A	101	1/8/07	1/8/07	1/9/07	1/15/07	1/22/07	1/29/07	1/30/07	2/2/07
"Talent Show"	101B	101	1/8/07	1/8/07	1/9/07	1/15/07	1/22/07	1/29/07	1/30/07	2/2/07
"Treasures"	102A	102	1/15/07	1/15/07	1/16/07	1/22/07	1/29/07	2/5/07	2/6/07	2/9/07
"I Wish I Was…"	102B	102	1/15/07	1/15/07	1/16/07	1/22/07	1/29/07	2/5/07	2/6/07	2/9/07
"Honor"	103A	103	1/22/07	1/22/07	1/23/07	1/29/07	2/5/07	2/12/07	2/13/07	2/16/07
"Daydreamer's Nightmare"	103B	103	1/22/07	1/22/07	1/23/07	1/29/07	2/5/07	2/12/07	2/13/07	2/16/07
"Give & Take"	104A	104	1/29/07	1/29/07	1/30/07	2/5/07	2/12/07	2/19/07	2/20/07	2/23/07
"I Dare You"	104B	104	1/29/07	1/29/07	1/30/07	2/5/07	2/12/07	2/19/07	2/20/07	2/23/07
"Busted!"	105A	105	2/5/07	2/5/07	2/6/07	2/12/07	2/19/07	2/26/07	2/27/07	3/2/07
"All's Fair…"	105B	105	2/5/07	2/5/07	2/6/07	2/12/07	2/19/07	2/26/07	2/27/07	3/2/07
"Perspectives" – Part 1	106A	106	2/12/07	2/12/07	2/13/07	2/19/07	2/26/07	3/5/07	3/6/07	3/9/07
"Perspectives" – Part 2	106B	106	2/12/07	2/12/07	2/13/07	2/19/07	2/26/07	3/5/07	3/6/07	3/9/07

Figure 4.1 – Production schedule 3 of 3

PREPARING FOR PRODUCTION SCHEDULE ISSUES

While a schedule needs to be efficient and cost-effective, always give some flexibility if problems arise, because production problems can vary and occur at any stage in the pipeline. Animated films have some advantage in this area because they are one large item that needs to be completed versus a series of episodes that must be delivered on a regular schedule. Also, it is becoming more commonplace to hold off announcing actual release dates until just weeks before debut, allowing for pushing back such dates if contracts allow. In television, regular delivery is expected to meet a broadcast schedule. Though the final products are shorter, more frequent delivery is required.

As to types of problems, a common one (not necessarily in frequency, but type) involves animation coming back incorrectly from overseas. If problems are few, they can usually be edited around or the overseas studio be asked to do a retake to edit in and replace the affected scene. However, if the problems are just too large or frequent, the episode may need to be held back until it can be corrected. This will, of course, change the episode airing order or film release date. Where this proves to be of specific concern is for television series that depend on the airing order to maintain continuity. The only choices (depending in large part on the distribution deal) is to run repeats until the episode is fixed and the story continues, or to skip the episode and proceed without it (either airing later in the first airing, or not appearing until second airing but in its normal spot). Other issues that may crop include: missed deadlines (such as with freelancers who are juggling too much and lose track of deadlines), scripts having to totally be rewritten for a variety of unanticipated reasons, and delays in approval of final models.

BUDGET AND VISION—WHEN SHOULD ONE COMPROMISE?

The heart of the matter comes regarding how strongly a producer wants to get a story to screen, and how much a producer feels can be accomplished with less money before people pay more attention to the inferior work than the tale being told. That said, it is undeniable that there will be some people out to simply make money, and to these producers any cost cut to raise profits will be perceived as acceptable. The more creative producer may feel that total quality must be used to preserve the final product, no expense barred, and putting full faith in the quality of the work paying for itself through critical acclaim, good word of mouth, and awards.

It really is a matter of each producer's personal tastes, as a general rule. There can, however, be exceptions. Such a case would be a "work-for-hire" where the hiring studio may provide some guidelines in this area that are expected to be followed.

As some examples of what is possible, here are some cost-saving measures producers can consider:

- **Use limited versus full animation:** The human eye can still process animation as movement even if the same drawing is copied for two consecutive frames before proceeding to the next motion; this process, best known as originating with Hanna-Barbera, is commonly referred to as "limited animation" or "animation on twos." Many animated television series historically take the "limited animation" route. However, if one does a project that requires a lot of fluid movement (such as elaborate dance numbers) or wants to do a feature film, "limited animation" will probably not meet production needs and the project will have to be what is called "full animation" or "animation on ones," where every single frame contains a different animated action.

- **Cut back on or disallow the use of flowing hair, draping cloth, busy patterns, or fur:** This primarily applies to 3D CGI but to an extent is also true in 2D cel animation, and the reasoning falls along similar lines to the use of limited animation. Anything that does not hold a solid shape requires extra animation to make it move credibly and not look jerky to the eye, and in the case of 3D CGI can be more time consuming both for the animator to set up and at the rendering stage. These items have to be done in great detail if done at all; otherwise, the resulting choppy quality can drag down the look of the whole production.

- **Try to have as many scenes as logically possible happen in as few locations as possible:** This cuts down on the number of backgrounds that need to be designed and ultimately animated, bringing cost savings at both the pre-production and production phases. However, the trick is making this high amount of location "reuse" transparent to the viewer. It should not call attention to itself and distract from the story that is trying to be told.

- **Use only a few extra characters to create the illusion of a crowd scene, not an actual large crowd:** Large crowd scenes are cumbersome for both character design and storyboard continuity. To only use a few characters cuts down on character design and animation because there are less people to draw, showing pre-production and production savings potential. However, this requires having competent storyboard artists on hand who know how to make good use of camera angles and staging so that the characters logically seem to mill around and aren't just completely recycled. A producer can offset some of this if one gives instructions for overseas to color the same background characters different ways to help them seem like different people, but that adds cost to the color department and can also create continuity confusion overseas if one is not careful.

WAYS TO CHART THE BUDGET AND SCHEDULE

There are two approaches to budgeting and scheduling a production. For the producer who doesn't mind the extra work, and at times loves figuring out how to tell programs to compute formulas, a word processing program (like Microsoft's *Microsoft Word* or Corel's *WordPerfect*) with a calendar feature and a spreadsheet program (like Microsoft's *Microsoft Excel*) can get the job done. These common formats can easily be read and shared by anyone on the production as needed. They also tend to be less expensive than specialized programs.

For those who prefer a full-service package that takes care of much of the guesswork, several options are available, but they don't necessarily come cheap. Of what is currently on the market as of this writing, Entertainment Partners offers *EP Budgeting* and *EP Scheduling* (with older editions known as *Movie Magic Budgeting* and *Movie Magic Scheduling*) tend to be the most commonly used programs in the business. Other programs on the market for budgeting as of this writing include *Showbiz Budgeting* (Media Services), *Axium Budgeting* (Axium), and *Gorilla* (Jungle Software). Alternate scheduling programs include *Reel Production Calendar* (Reel Logix).

HOW TO FIND OUT WHAT EVERYTHING COSTS

The best way to get a projected handle on production costs is to call around and get quotes from various potential production services. While time consuming, there are several key benefits to this approach. Of primary importance is access to the most up to date rates. Also, the producer by virtue of the personal contact makes his or her name known around town as someone actively in production, thereby increasing the professional network.

There software packages exist that break down the costs of labor for a number of entertainment services. Many of these are even designed to integrate with the budgeting programs previously discussed. Software packages at the time this was written include the *Showbiz Labor Guide* (Entertainment Publishers), *Showbiz RateMaster* (Entertainment Publishers), and the *PayMaster* (Entertainment Publishers). Each package has application to specific areas of the business. Also, bear in mind that none of this in the area of labor serves as a substitute for a labor relations attorney.

SPOTLIGHT INTERVIEW

ROBERT WINTHROP

Robert Winthrop comes from years of experience as a producer for animation. His credits includes animation for SD Entertainment (*Make Way for Noddy, Alien Racers, My Little Pony* specials), Netter Digital (*Max Steel*), and was involved in setting up the New York studio behind the Cartoon Network hit *Courage the Cowardly Dog*. Here, he talks a little bit about funding and budgeting.

"One way to get funding is to send or pitch your project to the studios in town. Most companies have a development department and are looking for new exciting projects. However, this is difficult as there are tons of projects out there and getting yours to stand out and be seen from the pack is difficult. On the chance that the studio likes the project they may want to do a development deal to flesh out the concept then move to production. Of course, the studios are not going to just give a person the money to produce the show. They may option the idea, do a development or production deal, etc. Another way is to contact studios in areas where co-production financing is the norm. Many Canadian companies like Studio B or Bardel, for example, have connections with TV broadcasters and through Canadian Government Subsidies can try to piece together the co-production financing for a project. Like pitching your project to a major studio this is not easy either as there are so many projects out there. I suppose another idea is to get your idea on the internet or out in the public somehow to try to create a buzz about it. Similar to *South Park* if enough people see the creative and like it someone in a position to make it happen in animation may see it and put together a deal. Of course visiting shows like NATPE or MIP are a good opportunity to see what types of projects are out there and to set up many meetings with companies in one place.

Each animated production is different so the budgeting must be tailored to accommodate these differences. How long is the production schedule, when does the project deliver, and how much staff will be needed to complete the project on schedule? Is the project 3d or 2d or a combination? Will there be heavy special effects compositing, etc. Type of project, TV, DVD, Feature? Quality and length affect the budget. Is the project based on a book or existing project? Or if it is original what is the creative? Will there be many characters, locations, vehicles? All of these questions affect the budget. Will the project be highly stylized requiring lots of art experimentation or a new untried style that will be difficult and time consuming to achieve? Some clients are more difficult to manage than others which may translate into production delays, additional staff to track approvals and meet deadlines. Music must be considered, too. Will the project include original songs, an orchestral or synth score? Voice talent must be considered. Will the project be going after celebrity voices or talent recorded in Vancouver? Even the director or producers assigned to a project may be a budget consideration if they are notorious for production delays or many creative revisions.

Companies like Disney are spending roughly $30 million for a direct to DVD movie and roughly $450 thousand per episode for a TV series. Nickelodeon is probably spending close to that for DVDs and $350 thousand for TV episodes. Small independent companies are doing DVD projects for $2 million and TV series for $250 thousand to $300 thousand. Obviously, there are big differences in how the projects are approached and the quality expected.

As far as overseas studios are concerned you can contact the studio and request a demo reel and list of projects. And many production studios will test overseas studios by asking them to do a small amount of animation for free to compare to other studios work. I think that meeting with the studio is important to connect on a personal level as well. But a word of caution that an animation test may or may not be a good representation of what the studio is actually capable of. Studios often attend MIP, the Kidscreen Summit etc., so this may be an easy way to meet with many studios at once. And of course industry publications like *Animation Magazine* will have information on this. There are of course trade shows, industry handbooks like *The Creative Industry Handbook* and many post production magazines. But in general asking around is the best way to find out about a studio. Much should be considered in addition to the price. Animation production is complicated and companies that have many years of experience are usually the better choices as they have seen more of the day to day production problems and know how to anticipate them and work around them. This is not to say that lower priced companies aren't good. The point is you have to balance price with experience and creative ability. I believe that you 'cast' production companies the same way you cast actors or voice talent. You have to look at all aspects in order to make the best decision.

Because each show has a different style or creative, a different staff, different clients etc., managing productions is always a challenge and different with each project. In some ways this is exciting and challenging. Of course previous experience helps tremendously in anticipating and managing potential problems but you can never anticipate everything."

SUMMING IT ALL UP

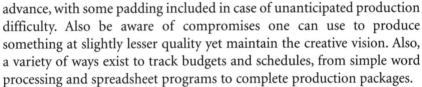

Financing, scheduling, and budgeting tend to be the most overlooked steps in a production. Awareness of the core audience that one wishes to reach is crucial before reaching out to potential financiers, in order to help solidify common goals, though it is quite all right for a program to reach beyond that core audience; the production just requires a sense of focus. Places to find reputable financiers and business partners include festivals and seminars, but one must be aware their time is limited and that follow-up will likely be required. Creative compromises may also be necessary with some financiers or business partners to achieve a partnership, based on cultural differences or individual tastes. Schedule pace must be anticipated in advance, with some padding included in case of unanticipated production difficulty. Also be aware of compromises one can use to produce something at slightly lesser quality yet maintain the creative vision. Also, a variety of ways exist to track budgets and schedules, from simple word processing and spreadsheet programs to complete production packages.

PART TWO:
Building the Team

CHAPTER FIVE

Meet the Players

GETTING TO KNOW WHO'S WHO

Animation cannot be produced in a vacuum. A producer must surround himself or herself with a strong team dedicated to getting the work done. This chapter provides overviews of the various people on an animation production crew, but generally speaking will not discuss a specific job in any detail. A detailed walk through the production process will come in later chapters. Also, remember to bear in mind that if one has decided to become a union production, some roles will be dictated by union guidelines. Also, bear in mind that if one chooses less traditional forms such as stop-motion animation (think *Wallace and Gromit* or *Chicken Run*), that there may be additional members on your team related to the model-making aspects of the process; those listed below tend to be more standard to the industry. Now, without any further delay, meet the animation team.

Line Producer

The Line Producer works with the creative producers to handle the day-to-day business aspects of a show. This includes the hiring and layoff of talent, scheduling, tracking of timecards and talent payment, and other high level administrative duties.

SPOTLIGHT INTERVIEW

MONIQUE BEATTY

Monique Beatty's Line Producer credits include *The X's, Catscratch,* and *Invader Zim* for Nickelodeon Animation, and *Mike, Lu, & Og* from Kinofilm. She's also been Associate Producer of *Extreme Ghostbusters* for Sony Animation (at that time Columbia-Tristar Children's Entertainment) and *Toonsylvania* for Dreamworks Television Animation. She shares some advice on how to manage the staff of a production.

"Always try to remember you get more with honey than you do with vinegar. I've heard that some Line Producers are just very... direct. They're not necessarily taking the artist's feelings into account—it's just,'You're late, I need it now.' It's not,'I understand you're late, how can I help you?' I think one of the big differences between artists and production staff is that—and I never remember which is which, right brain or left brain—they're one, we're the other. And so they look at things and think of things in a context of things specifically different than ours. We look at things in time and a linear fashion and calendars, and they look at creating something and they're done when they're done. Trying to find a happy medium between they're done when they're done and 'I need it now.' Artists work in a more visual world or more visual medium.

With my staff, rather than just hand them a storyboard and say it's due in three weeks, I hand them a storyboard page that had a cover with a master calendar on it that shows you should be done with your roughs at this point, you should be done with this at this point, and this is when you're all done. That way they can go through it every day and see the deadline in front of them. It's kind of a very simple thing, but it worked really well and it helped them meet their deadlines.

The smaller the studio, the better the interaction. I worked for Kinofilm. I think probably there were seventeen of us, so if an artist had a question or an issue or a problem, they could go to me, or they could go to the owner of the studio, because he was right down the hall and there was no set in stone corporate hierarchy. Everybody did whatever needed to be done. The bigger you get, the more compartmentalized everyone becomes.

I don't think the artist is involved enough in the preliminary process of development. They're obviously involved when they're creating the characters, they're creating the environment, they're creating the look of the show but no one ever sits down with the director or the storyboard artist and says, 'Hey, we're thinking of doing thirteen episodes and having each one be in a different location and our production schedule is really tight and we only have four weeks to storyboard and design each episode, and we have a very small budget.' Any artist would tell you, 'Are you crazy? You can't do that, this is going to look terrible.' Or 'If you do that, then do this.' I think that their input could be very valuable and I think that yes, it's important—production people obviously put together the schedule and the budget on the show, but with input like that from artists before your budget is set, before your schedule is locked in place, that's when you should be talking to them to say 'Is this feasible?' Or 'In your experience what happens if we do this?' Because every director I've worked with and every producer who's come up on the artistic side will look at the budget and the schedule and their first comment is usually, 'Who on earth put this together?' or 'What were they thinking?' or 'This is impossible.' There's always an amount of eye-rolling going on, and it's legitimate eye-rolling."

Production Manager (a.k.a. Associate Producer)

As mentioned in the interview, a Production Manager (or Associate Producer) also becomes very hands on in the administration of a production. A Production Manager reports to a Line Producer who may be responsible for one or several projects. That Line Producer will delegate out which responsibilities the Line Producer wants the Production Manager to handle on his or her behalf. Therefore, the exact responsibilities of a Production Manager vary from production to production.

Writer

There may be one or several writers involved on the animated project, regardless of whether it is for television or a feature (there may be a writing team on an animated feature, for example). The Writer works on crafting the specific details of the story, under the guidance of the producer's notes and also the Story Editor in the case of television. Of all the positions, the writer most likely will be the one who spends the least time on-site. These days, Staff Writers are not common and most are freelance (work off-site), which even often holds true for Story Editors.

Story Editor

A Story Editor (or multiple Story Editors) only enters the picture when working with an animated television series. His or her goal is to keep the story vision of the series focused, and correcting other writers' scripts as required, while freeing up the producer to focus on other matters. A Story Editor will regularly keep a rapport with a producer to keep the producer apprised of what new pitches have come in, the progress each approved script idea is making, and problems that occur during the writing process that may delay a finished script (or, at worst, prevent it from seeing completion). In turn, a producer communicates to a Story Editor which ideas for episodes meet the producer's vision and will be accepted to be written as scripts, and also of production issues that will require either the modification of scripts in process or completed scripts to meet these production demands (again, in the worst case, having to 'kill' a script because it cannot be produced for either budgetary or content reasons). Depending on the production, Story Editors may or may not be in-house staff.

Script Coordinator

A Script Coordinator makes sure that all edits done to a script remain incorporated in every phase of the process, reflecting the evolution of the story until a final, 'As Aired' version results. Not only does this include capturing version changes due to producer notes and revisions, but changes made to dialogue during the recording session, any subsequent pickup lines that may be done, and dialogue alterations made in the editing process. This is important because the 'As Aired' script will go to the closed captioning facility if needed, and also to foreign markets that need a base to translate to create their own versions. The Script Coordinator may or may not coordinate the distribution of the 'As Aired' copy (that may be left to the Post Coordinator), depending on the size of the production. However, the Script Coordinator almost always prepares the recording script for the voice actors, which must be specially formatted with line numbers for quick and easy reference to find a place in a script or to easily call for pickup lines. This position usually will be a staff role even if Writers and Story Editors are all freelancers.

Business and Legal Affairs

Especially for an independent producer, someone in business and legal affairs (whether in house or an outside consultant) is a must. Even though there are software packages and other resources for doing one's own contracts, the fine points of labor law make it a risky business to handle alone, especially if a producer never has done so before. Then there are additional issues, such as copyright and making sure a production company can obtain clearance to use names, locations, and other areas that are not created by the production. Once the producer adds in the decision to be a union production, and needing to make sure the union requirements stay followed to the letter, a producer probably is better served by surrounding him or herself with someone who can juggle this on a day to day basis.

Director

Sometimes also categorized as an Animation Director or Technical Director, depending on the demands of a production, this position guides that all the art elements of the production (models, storyboard staging, etc.) come together as a cohesive visual whole.

SPOTLIGHT INTERVIEW

JOHN GRUSD

John Grusd's credits include animated television, direct-to-DVD releases, and features. His career in the field began as a Graphic Director at Filmation on shows such as *He-Man, She-Ra,* and *Fat Albert.* Then he later moved to DIC where he directed shows including *The Legend of Zelda,* several incarnations of Mario Bros., and *Sonic the Hedgehog.* After that, John built a successful relationship with the heads of MGM Animation (here he directed several seasons of the *All Dogs Go To Heaven* show), and went on to work with them when they later formed their own company, SD Entertainment. Here, he talks about working with the director.

"Ideally, the producer and director work as a team. Each should have their distinct day to day responsibilities without much overlap other than the common goals of production. In that respect, the director and the producer can and should work closely. By the way, there are plenty of producer/directors in animation, including me. A good producer builds the framework within which the director operates. Nearly every decision the director makes is a creative one. That is the director's job. Because of the complexity of putting together many series productions, the plot greatly thickens when it comes to producers. As we have seen at the Academy Awards, the title of producer is less well defined. People who work for the rights holder get a producer credit. People who work for the client get a producer's credit. The production house itself has executive producers, producers, and associate producers. All of these producers have responsibilities unique to where they are coming from, and generally, all give some sort of notes on some aspect of the production. Inevitably, there are quite a few instructions from the producer(s) that the director must follow. A good director knows that this is part of the job and takes it in stride. It is not necessarily a bad thing.

A director needs to know how the production line works and how his/her decisions ripple through that process. I also worked in many capacities throughout the animation process which gave me an understanding of the artistry and detail of the animated art form. It is a complicated process that always seems as though the odds have conspired against a successful finish. Still, we manage to think our way through to the end. Also, and I can't emphasize this enough, it is always a wonderful experience working with the artists involved with the project. It's like magic being performed right in front of your eyes every day."

Storyboard Supervisor

Most productions seem to have a Storyboard Supervisor regardless of size of the crew. This person takes responsibility for making sure that all storyboards (whether parts of a movie or individual episodes) stay consistent for the visual quality of the show. This includes choices of camera angles and shots more so than art quality, since the process of storyboards more is about choreographing the action than being on model. The Storyboard Supervisor also handles the assignment of all storyboards in both the rough and cleanup stages, making sure as much as possible that artists get the episodes or portions of a film that best suit their skill set.

Storyboard Artists

There are two stages to storyboard artists: rough and clean-up artists. Someone who understands cinematic principles but may not be able to draw the "on model" does carry value as a rough storyboard artist, as the goal of storyboards is to provide a cinematic blueprint of how characters interact in the world as the story unfolds. That said, a rough storyboard artist has to be able to output at least fairly recognizable (even if not detailed) characters, props, and layout. The clean-up artists then go through and try to bring these images as close to on-model as possible, plus make any corrections that may need to be implemented from the notes of producers and others.

Art Director

Dependent mainly on production size, some productions have an Art Director to whom the heads of the character, prop, and layout departments report (as well as the head of the effects department, if utilized). This is to make sure that all these major areas maintain a consistent look and style between them to interface seamlessly. On smaller productions, the heads of these areas may report directly to the producer for this feedback and guidance. Art Directors oversee not only the creation of the main model pack (which apparently at Disney can also be referred to as the "999 pack") of stock items, but also of new material created for each episode.

Layout (Background) Artists

The groundwork for an animated world must be laid so a stage exists for the story to unfold upon. Every location comes to life at the hands of a layout artist, who may be called on to create anything from a realistic looking world to the incredibly fantastic. Layouts are usually done as wide shots of the environment, to allow for a large frame of reference for storyboard artists, animators, and colorists. If a specific item in a layout must be manipulated or used in the course of a story, it will often also be drawn as a prop in consultation between the layout and prop departments.

Character Artists

Animation, aside from the voice actors, does not have casting calls. The physical look of every character, from main star to bit player, must be designed by a character artist. These characters can range from humanoid, to animal, to protoplasm and anywhere in between. There usually exists a lead character artist, who either directly plays a great role in setting the character style of the production by originating the look or adapting the look of an existing property, or works with a producer that has art skills to be able to recreate the producer's art style (in order to allow the producer to concentrate on other areas). Each character must be drawn in three major ways: a ¾ front turn, a ¾ rear turn, and a side view. Straight on front and rear views are not done as many subtle details are lost in these views, and the ¾ views can be used as suitable reference for these positions as all the design information is provided.

The character models (as does any model sheet) serve a variety of purposes. First off, the existence of the model sheets allow for a consistent frame of reference for all storyboard artists and animators working on the production; otherwise, the style could vary widely. Secondly, it provides a single piece of artwork for the color department to mark up how to properly color each character. Lastly, if revisions need to be made to a character's look, this provides that only the model need be changed (in most cases) versus needing to change every storyboard panel.

There also exists a category known as Special Characters and Poses. As characters cannot just run to a wardrobe room and change such as real living actors can, a new version of a character must be drawn for each different outfit. The character must also model the outfit in the major positions ($3/4$ front, $3/4$ rear, and side view) to make sure the storyboard artists and animators stay consistent and accurate with the design. Also, it allows the color department to provide full coverage on how the outfit should be colored from any angle.

Prop Artists

Every little item a character needs to use, be it for one scene or an entire story, needs to be designed. Props include not only items that can be held, but any item that a character can manipulate or use. Vehicles, for example, are a specialized prop category.

Just drawing the props into the storyboard and having the animators use that for reference is not reliable for several reasons. First and foremost, if the storyboard has been split among several artists, each will very likely envision the same prop differently. Having a prop designer create each item ensures all storyboard artists work from a single reference in a consistent style with an approved look that also serves as a guide for the animators. Also, if revisions to a prop are required, only the single model need be changed instead of every frame of the storyboard in most cases. It also provides a separate item that can be passed on to the color department to be worked on without waiting for finished storyboards, thereby making more efficient use of time and talent.

Effects Artists

Effects artists join the team on productions where such things as laser beams, magic wands, dimensional gateways, and even lightning from the sky require a very stylized look and feel; in other words, they are usually utilized on science fiction and fantasy material. Drawings must also be designed in consultation with the producer to show storyboard artists and animators how the effects work step-by-step, to ensure that the effects stay consistent throughout the production not only in color and style, but in animation speed and overall duration of the effects. Therefore, a good Effects Artist also needs a keen sense of animation timing, especially if the producer has deputized the Effects Artist to generate most of the material. On a production with a small amount of effects demands, either the Art Director or an art skilled producer can generate any such required drawings.

Voice Director

Unless the producer's intent is to produce a picture where the action does all of the talking, most animated productions include the spoken word to varying degrees. These spoken words, called dialogue, must be overseen by a single individual responsible for making sure each character stays consistent in sound and true to the project. In order to free up the producer to concentrate on other issues, a Voice Director comes on board to work with the overall Director on handling this area of the production.

SPOTLIGHT INTERVIEW

MICHAEL DONOVAN

Michael Donovan's animation voice directing credits encompass a wide variety of projects, including the feature film *Heavy Metal 2000/ FAKK 2*, television episodes of *Martin Mystery, Noddy, War Planets* (a.k.a. *Shadow Raiders*), *ReBoot*, and the *He-Man and the Masters of the Universe* revival, direct-to-videos such as *My Little Pony, Max Steel,* and *Candyland* and the *Scary Godmother* television specials. He also held voice casting responsibilities on many of these projects, plus holds additional credits voice directing video games such as *The Hulk 1* and *The Hulk 2*. In addition, Michael's voice has been heard as a series regular on animated shows like *Mucha Lucha, Coconut Fred's Fruit Salad Island, X-Men: Evolution,* and *The Book of Virtues*. He shares some advice on working as a voice director.

"The voice director's job is to get the script that has been written, recorded in preparation for animating. The director works directly with the voice actors to get the best possible performance. I also work directly with the recording engineer to get the best possible recording. It's sort of like being a coach. He's not out on the field, but he provides the direction for which way the players should go.

I make sure that I read over the script carefully, giving attention to any extra sounds or added lines that need to be put in. I mark these on the script ahead of time, giving the additional info to the actors in the session. By reading the direction from the writer, I make sure that the actors are delivering the essence of what the writer intended. I make sure that we have the right guest characters. In a cartoon show, we always have the regular cast. But in every episode there are 'guest' characters that appear. I usually bring in people that I know can do the job. I make sure I am totally familiar with all characters, so everyone knows what they are supposed to be doing.

Some producers are easier to work with than others... but I try to make sure to advise them of my feelings and ideas while still acknowledging that they are the owners of the project. What usually makes things easier is to have many conversations before and during the casting process, so we both are on the same page.

I think what I enjoy most, other than being at the controls, is going into a studio … casting a show … picking all the actors … then going back in and recording the show or series, then after everything else has been done … seeing the finished product and being proud of the effort that everyone has put in … That to me is the greatest reward. The money doesn't hurt either. The most challenging thing for me is helping actors to rise above their level of comfortability. By that I mean, pushing actors to be better than they think they already are. Actors have very fragile egos, so you have to help them to attain a higher standard, while keeping their egos intact."

Casting Director

The Casting Director becomes hired specifically to locate the actors who will fill the spoken roles on the project. Sometimes the Voice Director may fill both roles, depending on production budget. More on casting will be covered in Chapter 7, "Pre-Production."

Voice Actor

A Voice Director's job is very ineffective without a group of talented men and women to bring the characters to life through vocal expression. These individuals, known as Voice Actors (regardless of gender), work with the Voice Director to achieve this effect. More detailed information about the voice recording process will appear in Chapter 7, "Pre-Production," where we will explore the role of Voice Actors further.

Recording Session Engineer

The recording session engineer makes sure that all the microphones are working and that sound quality is maintained by keeping the dialogue level (even). This is not to say that the engineer rides the potentiometer ("pot" for short, as it is more commonly known) on the sound board to keep the dialogue at a constant volume; after all, in the natural course of conversation some things will always sound higher or lower. The engineer makes sure the sound keeps that natural consistency and also that the recording remains free of technical difficulty.

Recording Session Dialogue Editor

After the dialogue finishes recording, an editor with the sound studio compiles the best takes into a single track, called the Normal Pause Edit. The name comes from the fact so that the Recording Session Dialogue Editor places a standard pause between each line of dialogue. A Normal Pause Edit sounds like listening to a radio play without music, effects, or crowd noises. More about the Normal Pause Edit, and how it will be used throughout production, will follow in later chapters.

Production Coordinator (a.k.a. Production Supervisor)

Drawing from my own experience, there seem to be two types of Production Coordinators: one that sees the show all the way through the pipeline, and the other devoted to a special need (Post, Script, or Color as examples). A general production coordinator helps shepherd an episode through the creative pipeline, allowing the other personnel (artist and non-artist alike) to concentrate on their individual roles. This was the kind of position I had on *Extreme Ghostbusters* for at Sony—though we were known as Columbia-Tristar back then—and would later hold on the *Say it With Noddy* interstitials, where I would actually also function in the Script and Post Coordinator capacities (as my position was non-union, that was allowable in that circumstance).

If errors are noticed, from inaccurate dialogue to incorrect models or storyboards, a Production Coordinator should not be afraid to at least inquire to the producer about them, and a producer should welcome the fact a Production Coordinator (or for that matter anyone) cares that much about the production's quality. Some may see the Production Coordinators or Assistants as simply glorified secretaries to the producer, but being in these positions is far more than just answering phone calls and scheduling meetings. More about this will be explained in upcoming chapters.

Production Assistant

This position does exactly as its name would imply—assist the production on whatever needs to be done. In the case of larger companies, sometimes there are Production Assistants that only manage office duties, and others that handle matters specifically related to the production pipeline. Examples of such pipeline-related duties include photocopying, cutting panels for animatics, and preparing packages for shipment. In smaller studios that do not maintain a separate designated runner or hire outside couriers, the Production Assistant may also serve in a runner capacity to take production related items wherever they need to be delivered.

Animatic Editors

An animatic (sometimes still referred to as a "leica reel," especially in Disney circles) consists of storyboard panels edited to an audio track. The purpose of this is to get a feel of how the finished picture will flow, a process to be further discussed in Chapter 7, "Pre-Production." Animatic editors need only digitally scanned storyboard panels, an audio track, and a video editing program that can run on a PC to get the job done. The ease of equipping someone to do the job (or finding a freelancer who can) allows for more hiring flexibility at this stage, reserving higher editing expenses for final footage.

Track Readers

Track readers listen to the normal pause edit and then break down the dialogue phonetically on the exposure sheet (x-sheet). This then gives a base for the lip assign person or team to work from. A track reader position usually serves separate from the sheet timers, unless the animations being produced are rather short and the sheet timer also has track reader and/or lip assign skills.

Lip Assign

People who do lip assign follow the dialogue and record for the animators what position to put the mouth in for each sound using a mouth chart, which shows a set of pre-determined positions for the face when a character speaks. At first, this might sound odd, but when the native language of the animators may not match the language of the piece being animated, it makes sense. As with a track reader, this position usually serves separate from the sheet timers, unless the animations being produced are rather short and the sheet timer also has track reader and/or lip assign skills.

Sheet Timers

Usually working under a designated Timing Director, though on smaller productions they may report straight to the Animation Director, sheet timers—also called "sluggers"—chart the course for the speed of the action by speaking in feet and frames of footage. For example, the average "walk cycle" (how long it takes most types of characters to make one step on screen, though if they naturally walk very fast or slow this will vary) is eight frames of footage, commonly denoted as "8x." Learning to at least read exposure sheets (commonly called "x-sheets") can be a valuable skill for a producer, though it will not be covered in detail in this book.

Checkers

Checkers do precisely what the name implies. These dedicated people are the last "eagle eye" pass all materials get before going overseas. They make sure that the storyboards and completed x-sheets match up in terms of action and lip assignment, as well as look out for any other unintentional errors on the storyboard (such as incorrect art panels or directional notes under the wrong panel).

Colorists

Colorists take the black and white models generated by the character, prop, layout (and effects, if required) teams and bring them to life in vibrant color. The color choices come from using a palette agreed upon in consultation with the producer. In addition to the standard colors, usually considered to be done in day lighting, the color department can be called on to "mark up" versions of the models in other situations (examples are night colors and firelight).

Overseas Supervisor

The Overseas Supervisor acts as an interpreter (sometimes literally, but definitely artistically) between the pre-production staff and an animation team that isn't local. This individual, familiar with the ultimate goals of the producer, makes sure that what the producer wants of the production becomes as clearly communicated as possible. This person works as the producer's eyes and ears elsewhere, since conference calls and emails cannot replace hands-on communication entirely. However, be aware some overseas studios can keep the relationship with an Overseas Supervisor strained and fight to keep them out of the process while others completely embrace the presence of an Overseas Supervisor.

Animators

Whether close to home or overseas, animators are absolutely key to any production. In some cases a producer may have more local contact with the animators (for example, in the case of Flash productions, animators may be able to kept closer to home because of the cost effectiveness), but generally they are only communicated with via video or audio conferencing and email. These are the people who use all the pre-production storyboards and model packs many others on the team invest their time and energy into, so a producer must make sure that the directions are clear so that the vision will be properly executed no matter how near or far a producer may be.

Ink-And-Paint

Digital painters do most of the "ink-and-paint" in the current animation process, though the occasional director still does traditional ink-and-paint for aesthetic reasons. Painters color each frame in the computer using software and devices such as art tablets. They color using the same standardized palette that the colorists selected overseas, with copies of the colored model sheets to help them make their artistic choices.

Video Post-Production Editor

As the animation becomes complete, finished scenes are sent to the post-production facility. There, the video post-production editor assembles the puzzle of footage. Also, the Video Post-Production Editor's responsibilities include inserting retake footage when poorly animated footage needs to be redone, and cutting out as few frames as possible to bring a production that has run over footage down to its proper length.

Telecine Operator

Since a project does not get consistent animators and digital ink-and-painters throughout, someone needs to take charge to see that color settings stay standard throughout the finished piece. This job, with traditional film, was done by the telecine operator, who made sure the struck film prints stayed consistent in the color process. With more of the video post process going digital, video editors sometimes take more control of the telecine process. However, there may be instances where the experience of a telecine operator is desired, especially if the producer wants to still use traditional film.

Post-Production Dialogue Editor

Once the video returns from overseas, the dialogue also must be edited to match any choices made with the final video. Also, any audio retakes must be dropped in, as well as any lines reused from elsewhere in the production (a different point in the film or other episodes). The last area that a Post-Production Dialogue Editor incorporates is the placement of wallas (crowd sounds) into the final dialogue track.

Foley and Effects

An animated world cannot fully come to life without the ambient sounds that make it feel "real." The sound of footsteps, lighting crashing, phones ringing, and even exotic unusual creature sounds in fantasy pieces all must come from these creative people. More specifics on foley and effects will be discussed in Chapter 8, "Post-Production."

Composer

Whether or not an animated piece has speaking characters, music is essential to making it work. Music sets the mood, punctuates action, and does so much more. Choosing a good musician who can complement the producer's vision is both a great challenge and a wonderful reward.

SPOTLIGHT INTERVIEW

CARL JOHNSON

Carl Johnson's composer credits for animation include both film and television releases. In the area of films, his work can be found as part of *Piglet's Big Movie, The Hunchback of Notre Dame II, Pooh's Grand Adventure, Aladdin and the King of Thieves,* and *The Return of Jafar.* His animated television credits include *Gargoyles, Alien Racers, The Mighty Ducks, Goof Troop, Pinky and the Brain, Animaniacs,* and *Batman: The Animated Series.* Here, he shares some details about composing and how music and film work together.

"When film and music work well together, the music acts as an emotional narrator to the action. The composer has to absorb the emotional impact of whatever is happening on screen and reflect it back to the listener in some kind of understandable musical way that will enhance the story. In this way the composer comments on the film as it progresses in the same way a narrator might comment on a story, leading the listener and highlighting important points. Beyond that, music for animation has to also emphasize the visual action that is happening on screen. By carefully considering the tempo, tone, and orchestration of the music, a composer can make an animated image seem heavier, lighter, faster, slower, and hopefully funnier. When the music is really working well for a piece of animation, it seems to give it a whole new dimension of life. In the same way our brains are able to observe a flickering succession of 30 pictures per second and create the illusion of movement, when we add music to those images it can create the illusion of life. By definition, animation is the process of creating an illusion that a series of static two- or three-dimensional pictures are actually moving. Perhaps animation music, then, is the process of creating the illusion that those pictures are really alive.

I think the best producers have a feel for when they need to micro-manage their production team, and when they need to let go and let their creative people do what they do. It is a very hard call to make sometimes, but the really great filmmakers can take a big view of their careers and realize that the whole world does not depend on the minute details of a particular scene. While there are some moments of any production that are more important, and need to be done right, there are also times when you need to trust others to do their jobs. Make sure there is adequate time for the composer to do his job. A good rule of thumb is that a competent composer should be able to write 90 seconds of music a day on average. When I can write three minutes in a day I'm thrilled. So for a feature with, for example, 65 minutes of music, you should allow the composer 45 working days. That never happens, of course, but as long as we're talking hypo-thetically we should be able to dream! Remember, also, that the more jobs the composer has to do, the more time it takes. In the best of situations the composer has a team of people to help him so that he can move quickly and concentrate on his job. When the composer also has to be music editor, orchestrator, copyist, performer, engineer and mixer, it makes things go much more slowly. Make sure that the creative 'chain of command' is clearly defined. Nothing is more frustrating for a composer than getting mixed messages from the creative decision-makers. A good producer can take the creative notes from a room full of competing egos and distill them down into a succinct set of instructions for the composer.

Formats will change. Whether it's 3-D, 2-D, hand-drawn, computer-rendered, HD or film, good animation comes from the skill of the animator, not from the technology he or she uses. Don't get caught in the trap that newer, better technology will give you a better end result. In the end, you still have to have a good story, good animation, and good music. As a mentor of mine once said, 'There is no substitute for quality.'"

SUMMING IT ALL UP

Though an animated production cannot happen without artists, it takes a dedicated and passionate team of people—artists and non-artists alike—to bring everything together. This chapter provides glimpses to all the players on the team to lay the groundwork for further chapters that take the production process step by step. Even if someone has a job on a production that a producer might never do his or herself, it behooves the producer to learn about every position to understand how to coordinate the pieces to make them work together in the most effective way.

CHAPTER SIX

The Challenges of Doing Business Abroad

LOCATION, LOCATION, LOCATION

Last chapter introduced the major players of an animation team. Now the question comes, especially in the case where multiple studios have become involved in production, is the location of these individuals and how it impacts creating the animated project.

DEALING WITH COMPANIES ON AN INTERNATIONAL SCALE

In some form or another, almost every production will need to deal with animation on a global scale. Even if a producer's been able to move forward without any other international financial partners, the odds are high at least part of the production will be outsourced. So thinking about how to deal with companies on an international scale should always be a consideration.

METHODS OF COMMUNICATION

Emails

Emails, especially with the increased ability of mobile devices to send and receive them, generally are industry standard for speaking with international partners and outsource teams. Scanned artwork can often be attached and sent as well (provided the file size is not too big, otherwise FTP must be used as described below), so more than words can do the talking. Convenience exists in that people can read it whenever they have a moment; however, that same luxury empowers people to make emails less of a priority for them even if the producer needs an urgent answer. The danger in email is that no sense of tone exists, so words tend to be read rather literally and if something can be misinterpreted one run the risk that it will; this risk becomes even greater when dealing with people for whom English may not be a first language. So make sure to think carefully before writing.

Fax

Faxes are becoming less and less common as email becomes more accessible globally, and also as it becomes easier to scan artwork to attach it to emails. However, in some cases, a fax may still be the quickest or most reliable method to relay art related notes to someone overseas particularly if that individual does not have their own dedicated email account. Having pointed that out, there runs a risk that the fax will distort the image, particularly when exchanging faxes between countries with letter paper and A4 paper size standards.

Teleconferences and Videoconferences

The main difference between a teleconference or videoconference comes in whether or not one can see the other parties involved in the call. The advantage comes largely in the ability to get multiple people together in one place for spontaneous collaboration or making sure everyone is on the same page if confusion occurs. Secondary benefits include The difficulty, however, comes in getting everyone together for a tele-conference or videoconference, especially when dealing with outsourcing companies; it may be hard to find a time that can work for everyone. Because of this, these kind of conferences tend to occur only rarely and cover the most essential of subjects.

FTP

The use of FTP (File Transfer Protocol) can be classified as a method of communication because it serves as the way to send files of information back and forth that are too large to simply attach to an email. Because so much of animation has gone digital, depending on the size of a retake (but it has to be very short), sometimes they can even be received digitally in this matter, and then burned to a disc to be provided to the post house. Until technology becomes better though, this is not recommended unless one is in a major bind, because it is still time consuming. The best use of FTP, at the time of this book's writing, would be to send low resolution polygon clips several minutes in length to producers to get a feel of how early production proceeds. Technology, however, could make it practical to send more of the final show this way over time.

THE LANGUAGE OF INTERNATIONAL COMMUNICATION

English seems to be keeping a foothold as a major business language. That said, do not assume that simply because everyone one deals with at a company knows English that they understand what is being said, because even under the language different cultural nuances and perspectives come to the table.

SPOTLIGHT INTERVIEW

LARRY DITILLIO

Larry DiTillio's credits include co-story editing the *Transformers* sequel series *Beast Wars,* for which the animation was produced by Mainframe Productions in Canada while he lived in the United States. He has also worked on productions with the French-based company Gaumont. He is also well known for his writing and Story Editor work on *She-Ra: Princess of Power.* He shares some tips on how to work with foreign producers.

"Foreign companies often have much more respect for writers, something most of us are not used to in the American industry. I was treated royally in both Canada and France and have many fond memories of both.

As a writer, your job is to be open and honest with your employers and try as much as possible to give them what they want. This includes dealing with cultural differences. One important thing is to not be too 'American' (even more so in today's world) in your approach. Remember even if foreign companies want to catch the American market their first concern is pleasing their home audiences. Many things which play well with American viewers do not play with foreign audiences. Comedy in particular doesn't always travel well. Likewise, politics. You simply can't go into a foreign company and present them with distinctly American forms of story-telling. Think globally!

Foreign producers are not looking to America for budding talents; they have plenty of those in their own countries. What they are looking for are writers who know a lot about their craft and about the American entertainment industry, usually with an eye to expanding their market to America.

To find foreign companies with offices in America and try to get meetings with as many foreign companies have offices (usually in L.A. or New York) and these companies are often more amenable to meeting with writers than the corporate giants running the American industry. Start with the trades, such as *Hollywood Reporter* and *Variety*, usually with contact numbers you can call and inquire to find out what these companies might currently be on the lookout for. Research the company any way you can. You should certainly be open to all opportunities and given the increasingly incestuous nature of the American industry, it might actually be easier to hook up with a foreign company."

OUTSOURCING

Why do it?

The producer may know people with certain sets of high-quality production skills. However, when a project finally comes together, this same producer may not hire these people (potential personal conflicts of interests notwithstanding) and instead contract with another company that may be in another country. This process is called outsourcing. The question then arises why a producer who knows about and has access to local talent would deal with individuals elsewhere.

The reality revolves almost exclusively around finance. A producer may not have sufficient funds to afford personnel in his or her own country, leaving little choice but to go abroad. Also, international co-producing partners or third-party financiers may end up stipulating (either themselves in the financing deal or by the laws where they are located) how the money must be spent and the labor allocated.

Also, even if some of the labor can be done by contracting with an entity in the country of origin of the producer, cases may arise that due to a tight timetable, the local crew cannot handle everything. Even in these cases, the work must be split up in order to meet these needs. Splitting up work between multiple entities, regardless of location, is known as subcontracting.

Remember that these definitions apply to making contractual deals with other companies where multiple individuals from that company do work on the production. They generally do not apply when discussing the hiring of individual freelancers, no matter where in the world they might be or if the individual freelancer is incorporated (such as a limited liability corporation). It is frequently possible to have storyboards, for example, where parts are assigned out to local artists and other portions sent by carrier service companies to artists elsewhere in the country or nearby countries (such as Canada, in the case of the United States).

Upsides

Cheaper labor: Generally speaking, the cost to a producer is less per dollar to produce the work in a country other than his own. This reflects more the condition of the local currency in relation to others and the local economy and not necessarily a reflection on the quality of the work that will be performed. So, as demands for footage increase, it becomes more affordable to outsource as more product is being received per dollar.

Round the clock workforce: Even if some staff members are located locally in-house, other factors (such as delivery dates) may dictate that others need to be at work elsewhere on a different time shift to meet the schedule. In this instance, a producer could stagger shifts between the in-house and overseas location so that as one group ends working for the day, the next one begins. The same principle can also be applied when coordinating multiple outsourced animation houses with no local team.

Downsides

The main downside of outsourcing is the loss of control because of the loss of supervision. Although a producer can do much with email, fax, and conferencing, the producer still cannot always physically be on site with the outsourcing company (though the producer may come over and visit several times during the course of the production). The choice of who gets hired on as Overseas Supervisor may very well make or break a production. This person, empowered to act on the producer's behalf, must be understanding of the feelings of the outsourcing company yet not too sympathetic towards them, as the first loyalty must remain to the producer and the producer's vision (possibly as defined by the producer and other financing partners).

What parts of the Production Usually Stay In House?

In a nutshell, there are several aspects of a production that tend to stay in house no matter what because of the need to control the vision. These are development, writing, art design, direction, and storyboards. Please note that the word "tends" starts off this list, because times exist that some of the writers and storyboards may be sent to people in other countries. However, the Story Editors and Storyboard Supervisors still remain as part of the core in-house team through which all items are then reviewed; in the case of a feature film, offsite writers generally report to one of the producers on the film.

BARRIERS IN DEALING INTERNATIONALLY AND HOW TO COMPENSATE

Culture Barriers: Language barriers can make directions hard to understand if the first language of the people the producer wants to communicate with is not the same as the producer's. Another area involves items in the script or storyboard which may raise cultural confusion or objections with people in other countries and in turn stall the production process, particularly if the Overseas Supervisor proves not to be effective as a mediator. A producer also needs to understand enough of the culture of any international companies being dealt with, in order to not make gaffes when communicating with representatives of these countries directly and to take items such as the international holidays into effect when creating the production schedule. That said, a producer must be careful not to become too sympathetic in particular to outsourcing companies or he or she may become less careful in enforcing deadlines.

Financial Barriers: Since the value of currency between countries does not usually remain steady through the life of a production, especially given the long timetables of an animation project, it can be challenging to stay on top of costs. Also, if a producer relies heavily on co-production monies, there remains a gamble in the fact the finances are not in the producer's control and something could happen to lose any international partner at any moment. Sometimes financial issues alone can kill what might have been an otherwise successful production.

Involvement Barriers: While involvement remains possible due to technology, the amount each entity participating in the production can be involved still remains guided by their proximity to the creative core. This may not even necessarily be in terms of physical location, but a matter of proximity to the decision making levels of the production. While a creative producer with the vision will certainly come out above an outsourcing "work-for-hire" company, the number of other international partners (particularly in the finance area) may place restrictions on how the producer can stand up for the property. Though, bear in mind, this same phenomenon can happen when dealing with multiple producers domestically as well.

BENEFITS IN DEALING INTERNATIONALLY

Gaining multicultural perspective: This benefit may not be readily apparent at first, in part because it grows out of the cultural barriers. However, the issues that arise when an overseas company (production partner or overseas outsourcing company) finds something they don't understand or potentially objectionable in the work helps give a good precursor of how international audiences could react, and as most producers wish to reach a global audience this is valuable feedback that might not have been received had the work completely been produced locally. Dealing with these issues now may prevent larger trouble if not caught before the piece is complete.

SUMMING IT ALL UP

Dealing internationally, whether for financing or production output reasons, seems to be a reality of the business to stay. Therefore, it becomes important for a producer to understand what barriers (such as cultural ones) exist between the companies they are trying to deal with outside of their own country, and what resources are at his or her disposal to combat these potential problems. That said, a producer must be careful to make sure that while remaining understanding, they also cannot become too sympathetic to the international companies they deal with or the risk is run that control of the production may erode from the points originally agreed upon.

PART THREE:
The Production Process

CHAPTER SEVEN

Pre-Production

ONCE THE STORY IS APPROVED

When a story finally gets down in a final form, whether it be as a full script or thumbnails with notes (more likely with shorts), it is time to move into the phase known as 'pre-production'. At first this may sound odd, because one would think that the project is always in a state of production until it is finished. In animation, the term 'production' in regards to the pipeline refers specifically to the phase where the story actually becomes animated. The phase before this is therefore 'pre-production,' and the assembly of the footage after is 'post-production' (both of which will be covered in other chapters).

The below process walks through what takes place when a full script is used as the starting story blueprint, as it is what I am most familiar with from my professional experience and is common. The process can be adapted using a thumbnail storyboard and otherwise stays the same as long as some starting list is generated as to what characters, props, background layouts, etc. are required.

Generally, the process described applies whether film or television episodes and being produced. The process also tends to be the same regardless of medium (i.e., 2D, 3D, Flash). Where minor differences exist, they will be pointed out.

BREAKING DOWN THE SCRIPT

As soon as the producer knows a script has been signed off on by all pertinent parties, it is ready to hand off to the Production Coordinator for a process known as "script breakdown." Basically, the Production Coordinator goes through the script with highlighter markers (designating one for each type of item) and indicates the first appearance of every model type in the script. This will give a sense of how many total models will be needed for a given production. The Production Coordinator then inputs the list of items into a program used for tracking the creation of model sheets and their progression through all steps of the process, from initial creation through final color markup.

What program is used can be something as complex as a proprietary program or as simple as a form generated by a spreadsheet program, though currently it is more common to use programs that allow for electronic drawings of models to be attached to listings that are also searchable like a database, and often these must be custom-designed. These lists then are printed out and provided to the director to know what is available to hand out to the storyboard crew. Lists can take on whatever form is most convenient to the production, but the most basic of lists reflect each model's name and the first scene in which each one appears.

CASTING AND VOICE RECORDING

A full view of what goes into casting and voice recording is beyond the scope of this book, but an overview of the process should at least provide a sense of what takes place. First, the producer hires a Casting Director and provides him or her with background information about the characters, including sample dialogue for each character, known as "sides." The Casting Directors distribute this information to agents and managers to find out who can provide talent that may fit these needs, and in turn receive "demo reels" highlighting the capabilities of potential actors or referrals of actors with whom the Casting Director previously has worked. Those that seem to best fit the need in the estimation of the Casting Director will then audition in front of the Casting Director and producer using the sides. From these auditions, the choices will be narrowed down until a cast is finalized.

In most cases, a ready script will be sent to each of the individual actors and they first meet in the recording studio for what is known as a "dry run." The one exception is some primetime animated comedies, that do bring all the actors together for a "table read" similar to live-action sitcoms. In this case, the writers do tweak the script as it is acted out and a modified version then is distributed for the actors to bring to the actual record. "Table read" situations are not common in animation largely due to the extra time and budget involved.

Not all actors for a cast may be at the main record session; in fact, there are some productions where each actor comes in individually and reads lines, either due to scheduling or to the nature of the production (this is specifically true of ADR where nothing is gained by actors "reading off" one another as each line must be read to lip sync and time). Even in a case where multiple actors read through a script together, individual lines may be repeated several times to try out different deliveries (acting) of the line, or variations of the line if the voice director or producer (depending on who is leading the record; in some primetime animation, the producer also takes on the voice director role) is not sure that the line as written is the best choice and wants to have several choices going forward in the production. It costs additional time and money for each session (studio rental, talent and crew time, etc.) so it behooves a producer to get as much material out of a single session as possible, including pick-up lines if additional or replacement dialogue becomes required for creative, technical, or legal reasons.

The final selections (called circle takes) from these sessions will be placed together back to back in their proper order with an equal amount of space between each line delivered. This is known as a normal pause edit, which becomes the beginning audio blueprint for the project. Normal pause edits are assembled by the voice director and sound engineer and then delivered to the producer in most cases, along with all pertinent notes, because the producer may not be at every voice record session. This is especially true in cases where the voices record in another physical location (i.e., city, state, or county) compared to the offices of the producer.

An important thing to note is how voice recording is handled in animated films versus animated television. In film, a "scratch track" initially tends to be recorded which consists of members of the staff acting out the roles, with the final dialogue by the professional actors to be edited in at a later stage. In television, the selection of actors and often the recording of the episode are completed before storyboards are drawn.

SPOTLIGHT INTERVIEW

JACK ANGEL

First distinctly known to animation fans as the voices of Hawkman and Flash for *Superfriends,* Jack's other memorable roles include Astrotrain, Ramjet, and Ultra Magnus from *Transformers* and Zarkon, Hazar, and Cossack from *Voltron: Defender of the Universe.* He's also provided his talents to additional voice ensembles for feature films such as *Cars, The Hunchback of Notre Dame, Toy Story 2,* and *The Iron Giant.* More recently, his credits have expanded to video games, including *EverQuest 2, Shadow of Rome,* and *Call to Duty 2.* Jack shares some of his experience doing voice acting.

"I was a disc-jockey for 18 years and I did funny voices on the radio. Then in commercials and finally I auditioned for and got the parts of Hawkman & The Flash on *Superfriends* at Hanna-Barbera. There's a great deal of professional status, great money, no effort, and I get to work with the best people in the business. I think you must have an agent. And a good one who's in the animation loop. Once in a while another actor will ask if I read for something or other and then I'll tell my agent and she'll check it out.

Guesting can be hard because you are not one of the regulars and they all have a show history that goes on while you're there and sometimes you never find out what the joke is. If you're a little insecure, that can be deadly. In *Transformers,* I only did one or two characters in each episode. And as some died off or were phased out, I assumed new characters. In *Voltron,* that was a Japanese cartoon first, so we just replaced the

Japanese dialogue with English. We 'wild-tracked' each line to time. It would take about a half hour per episode and we would do all of one character's lines and then all of the next. *Treasure Planet* was done more like *Voltron,* except we were on a looping stage at Disney and recorded sometime to picture and sometimes before there was any picture.

People will tell you, 'You can't do that.' You can. Everyone doing it is just somebody who didn't listen to the nay sayers. Run with the hounds at your heels. Take chances. And don't believe the myth that this business is filled with rejection.

Casting people are in the business of 'selecting' and the way they do it is by seeing a bunch of people and choosing *one.* Nobody got rejected, somebody got selected. Your turn will come if you just keep going back and working you make yourself better at your craft."

MODEL SHEET CREATION

As the recording process goes on—usually somewhat before—artists work under the guidance of their respective Supervisors, using the lists generated by the Production Coordinator during the script breakdown process, to create drawings all the needed items for the production. This includes characters, props, background layouts, and effects (if the show warrants them), which collectively are known as model sheets.

Do not forget that even the 3D animation process begins with 2D model drawings and storyboards. I heard it said once at a professional get together something along the lines of "the 2D guys control it all" which was not meant as a gripe but an observation. 2D and 3D animation begins from the same conceptual roadmaps, but it is just that 3D animation takes a different turn at a certain point in the production process. What follows is an in-depth look at the major model types.

MODEL TYPES

Characters (and Special Poses)

As discussed in Chapter 5 ("Meet the Team"), character designers usually design characters in three major poses: the ¾ front, ¾ rear, and a side view. Between these three angles, all the necessary character details emerge, as a straight on front or rear view provides no additional information (and in fact may provide less than a ¾ view). Also, as mentioned before, since characters cannot just go and change clothes from an existing wardrobe, every time they need to wear something not part of their usual attire, this must be a separate design known as a Special Pose or Costume.

To clarify, however, Character is a section where any living creature is filed. If our sample character fends off a snake in the jungle, the snake is considered a character. If she swats away a fly, the fly is also a character. This is because the fact they are living means they can have attitude and expression while interacting; this attitude therefore brings about character. To illustrate the difference between Characters and Special Poses, the next two pages feature two different pieces of character artwork for the sample character. The first (Figure 7.1) shows her standard turnaround. Figure 7.2, by comparison, shows her in an outfit that she does not usually wear in the series—thereby qualifying it as a Special Pose or Costume.

Figure 7.1 – Sample Character Turnaround

Figure 7.2 – Sample character in a Special Costume

Mouth Chart

In order for the track reader to be able to properly show how a character "speaks," a code must be established between the studio and the animators to know how the mouth should be positioned for each sound. Due to the varying facial structures of characters, it is practically impossible to have a "one size fits all" kind of pattern that will automatically be understood and able to be applied across the board. This specialized code of mouth movements is established visually by using something known as a "mouth chart," where the character's mouth is shown in each of the various positions and a letter assigned to each position. Because some letters sound similar, the same mouth shape can be used for multiple letters. Generally less than a dozen mouth shapes are found on any given chart.

Expressions

To get a sense of how a character should move and act, a series of looks and poses are drawn. These are usually referred to as Expressions and are done for the main characters as part of the main model pack for the major characters and sometimes high-level secondary characters as well. Expressions generally are not done for every character.

Size Comparison

One of the biggest challenges, especially with a newer show, comes from having no sense of scale. Without some frame of reference, artists and animators cannot determine how tall various characters should be next to one another. Therefore, it is common practice for shows to have a Size Comparison (known as "size comp" for short) of the main characters standing next to one another to help keep things standard.

Size comparisons can also be very crucial between characters and certain props. Imagine for example if a lead character regularly drives a certain kind of car. A producer wants to make sure the animators always draw the lead character the right size so as not to be too big or small for the car! A real life example of this comes from early in my career, on *Jumanji*. The episode had Van Pelt the hunter wanting to capture the boy Peter in a cage, but the joke is that Van Pelt gets caught. My first day or so was right when this episode shipped and they asked me to size comp the cage... to Peter. I hadn't been able to read the script to realize the cage really should have been compared to Van Pelt, so what we got back as a Take 1 from overseas was an absolute mess as they tried to figure out how to put an adult man in a tiny cage! Unfortunately, the studio had to pay for the retake, but fortunately, everyone saw how the mistake got made and I kept my job. This shows the importance of everyone knowing the context of a script regardless of position on a show.

On the next page, the sample character appears in a Size Comparison lineup (see Figure 7.3) with other characters she will interact with.

[Figure 7.3 – Size Comparison of the sample character with several other characters]

Effects

Effects may or may not be important at the storyboard stage, depending largely on the nature of the project. A production set in an environment requiring futuristic looking gadget fire or magic effects will want to set those standards early on to make the visual tone of the show clear and cut down (if not completely eliminate) room for error. Nature effects, such as flames or floodwater waves, may be easier to just have the storyboard artists draw very generically at this stage and then customize any stylized look and feel with the overseas studio.

Layout

Since characters can't be taken on location, locations must be "brought to them" through the skills of talented Layout artists (also referred to as Background artists). Each needed area is drawn in a wide shot including all areas where action will take place in a given setting, if possible, though sometimes multiple angles of a larger location need to be created. If close-ups shots are required to be drawn in storyboard or animation, it is assumed that the artists or animators can refer to this wide shot and draw accordingly.

Figure 7.4 - Location Layout Artwork

Figure 7.4 shows a location that the sample character might appear in for a story. Note the use of shadow tones.

Props

Every character interacts with inanimate objects as part of a story. These objects are collectively called props, and can be of anything. A box of cereal, an umbrella, futuristic space weapons, are just some types of items. If something doesn't clearly fit any other category, Prop tends to be the catch-all place to put it. This also includes items that might otherwise be part of a background layout, but because the character has to interact with them (such as breaking a branch of a tree, because one has to not only show the tree but how the branch looks separate from the tree) this will require them being on a separate level of animation and therefore no longer part of the background.

Figure 7.5 shows a sample prop with a hand showing size comparison.

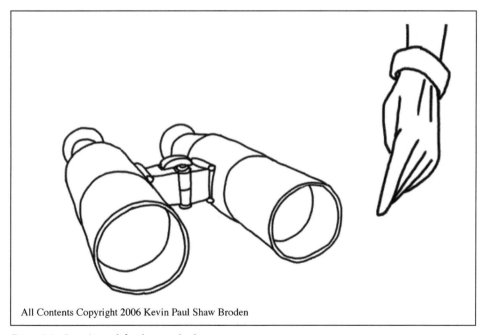

Figure 7.5 – Prop Artwork for the sample characters

Vehicles

Vehicles are usually treated as part of the prop category, and not broken out with any sort of special labeling. However, unlike other props which may show only one view, vehicles always have at least a ¾ front and ¾ rear view. Also, it is common to show a Size Comparison of the Vehicle to the character who usually operates it to get a sense of scale.

Figure 7.6 shows a Size Comparison of the sample character to a Vehicle.

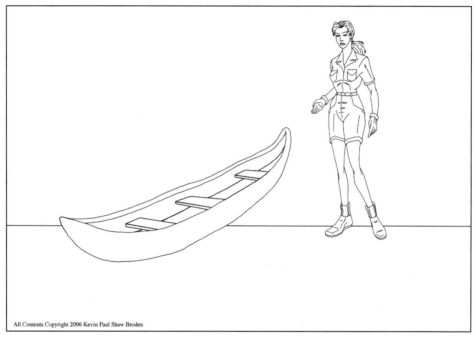

Figure 7.6 – Vehicle Artwork Size Comp for the sample character

"PASTING UP" THE MODELS ONTO SHEETS

As each model becomes completed and ready to go for approval, the original drawings (or copies of the files) are given to the Production Coordinator to be "pasted up" on to model sheets. The term "paste up" comes from the fact that in the beginning, the models (preferably photocopies of them) would be cut out and fastened using removable tape to a standard template. This standard template—known as a model sheet—contains the production's name, the episode name (in the case of a television series), an identification of the type of model shown on the page (e.g., prop, character), and the model's name and corresponding code number. These days, the act of assembling a "paste up" can be done seamlessly and digitally, by copying a model out of one file on to the standard digital template in another file where all the pertinent information can be simply typed in.

THE REFERENCE PACK OR STYLE GUIDE

For some shows, the director and the producer (if an art producer, this will tend to be more hands on) come up with a visual guide of how they want staging to be done throughout the production. This can include desired shot angles, illustrations of how to light and shade scenes for best intended effect, and more. This can be called either a reference pack or style guide, depending on the studio, but they are the same.

ALL THE INGREDIENTS FOR A STORYBOARD

All the models (while also good reference for the animators) ultimately serve as the building blocks to create the storyboard, which is the cornerstone of the animation process. All other phases of the process hinge in some way upon the storyboard, all the way through post production. After the rough main models become agreed upon, packs of character, props, backgrounds, and "normal pause edit" tapes are sent to storyboard artists. Unlike model artists, who tend to handle all phases of creation, storyboard artists (except in rare cases) divide into two key specialties: rough and clean-up.

Rough storyboards

In a rough storyboard, concern revolves around staging over art quality. Artists doing rough storyboards better need to understand cinematography than being able to draw on model, though their models should at least be discernable. This includes fundamentals such as where not to cut off characters in a camera shot and the psychology of the camera behind using an upshot on a character versus a downshot on the same character. Not having fully detailed storyboards at this stage in the game allows for relatively quick corrections if plot or staging problems arise, without a lot of lost time and effort. Because of the amount of creative freedom allowed, within the realm of the guidelines laid down by the Storyboard Supervisor, Director, and Producer, being a rough storyboard artist carries with it a level of responsibility.

Cleaned-up storyboards

Clean-up storyboard artists specialize in exactly what the name implies. Their job is to get all the characters, props, and locations as "on-model" as possible. Some clean-up artists remain at doing this because it is what they enjoy doing; for others, being a clean-up artist is the "breaking in" level and if good cinematographic sense is shown, he or she may be promoted to a rough storyboard artist.

PARTS OF A COMPLETED STORYBOARD

A completed storyboard consists of four major components: panels, camera instructions, dialogue and sound effects, and timing.

- **Panels:** Panels lay out the pictures that tell the story. The most key poses for the animators are shown, not only to convey a continuous sense of action but to also lay the minimal framework for the animatic (also known as a leica reel, to be discussed later in the chapter). Scene and panel numbers appear at the top of each panel. A change in scene number indicates an abrupt change in camera angle, while when the camera follows someone around this remains part of the same scene; panel numbers indicate that all of these frames belong to the same piece of action in the same camera shot or move. Notations appear between panels to indicate important visual changes, such as cuts between scenes with triangular symbols between panels. When it needs to be made clear that the next scene is not a change of location but rather continues the action from the prior scene, the letters HU are put in a circle between the two panels to indicate a "hook up" between the scenes.

- **Camera Instructions and Action Description:** Though the panels should clearly convey the camera instructions, they are repeated here as an added measure in the first row of information below the panels. Also, any description related to the action in the frame appears here as well so that the animators know the context of the story and what is expected to take place. This also helps address any potential ambiguity that might exist in the storyboard that cannot be avoided despite the most careful staging.

- **Dialogue and Sound Effects:** Often reduced on a photocopier taken directly from the script, these are cut and pasted into the middle row of the storyboard.

- **Timing:** Animation footage translates to feet and frames, and even though so much is digital animation-speak still uses the language of film which is 24 frames per second. Timing information on a slugged storyboard can be found as the last row of information. Discussing timing in depth lies beyond the range of this text, but there are a few general guidelines. The average character walk cycle (the motion it takes for a character to take a step putting one first in front of the other), for instance, is 8 frames of film; this means that in one second of screen time a character will move one foot, put the other foot in front of it, three times. Dialogue is timed simply by putting the letter "D" in the box below the corresponding panel; if additional action happens during the panel, it can be listed as dialogue plus the frames required (e.g., D + 8x). When a panel consists solely of frames it can be written 8x or 0^{08} (with the large 0 meaning feet and the superscript number representing frames), but once a single panel exceeds 23 frames, then it must be written in the feet-and-frames format.

On the following pages, Figure 7.7 features a completed five page cleaned-up storyboard sequence featuring the sample character.

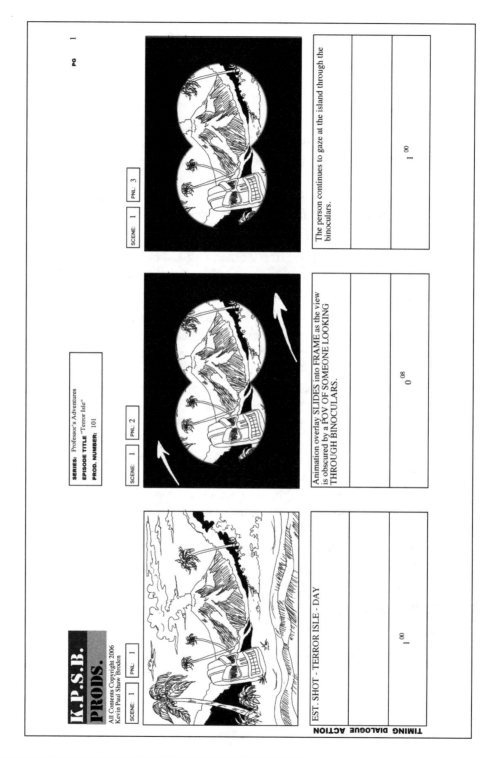

Figure 7.7 – Sample Storyboard Sequence

Figure 7.7 – Sample Storyboard Sequence

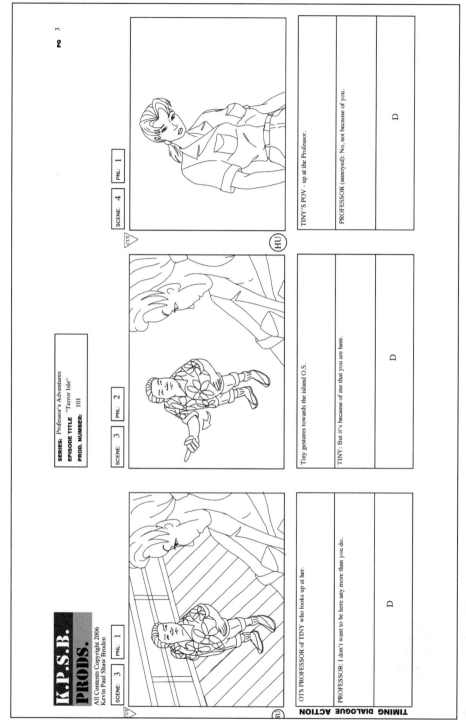

Figure 7.7 – Sample Storyboard Sequence

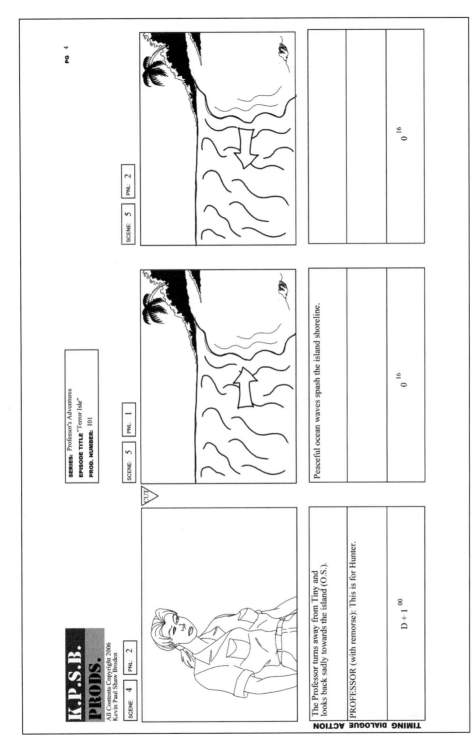

Figure 7.7 – Sample Storyboard Sequence

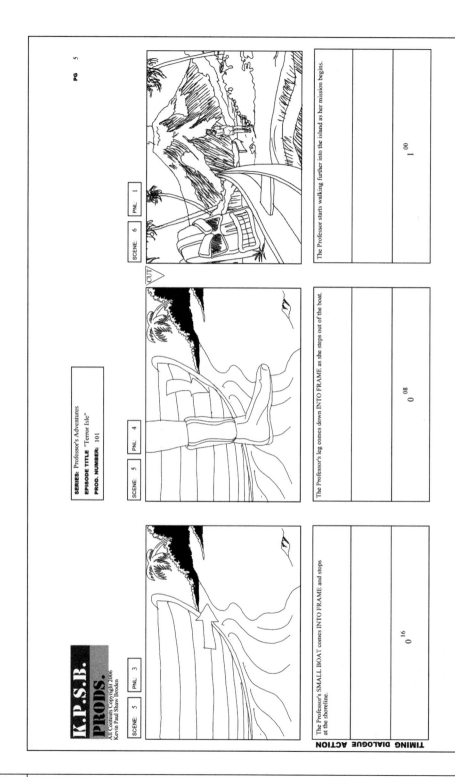

Figure 7.7 – Sample Storyboard Sequence

THE ANIMATIC (OR LEICA REEL)

Once all the scenes are drawn for a storyboard, an animatic (also known as a "leica reel" at some companies) editor scans the panels and assembles them digitally to the normal pause edit track. Depending on the production workflow, rough timing for the animatic will either be determined by the director sitting with the animatic editor, or (more usually) the animatic editor will guess at a rough timing to then be adjusted by the director. This timing becomes noted in pencil at the bottom of the storyboard; it must be in pencil because timing will continue to be adjusted until the project is complete.

After the director feels satisfied with the quality of the animatic, he or she brings it to the producer and other parties that must sign off to screen the completed product. This happens either collectively in a meeting or sending them tapes to view and then comment on. From these evaluations inevitable arise notes, that may be as simple as just changing some timing for certain panels of the animatic but more often than not result in storyboard revisions (either because issues are revealed at this stage that were not apparent simply viewing a printed page, or more material must be added for timing considerations). Then the editing and screening process repeat until all interested parties sign off on the animatic as approved.

TRACK READING, TIMING, LIP SYNC AND CHECKING

With the animatic signed off on, the project moves on to the track reading stage. Basically this involves someone listening to the normal pause edit and laying out the dialogue phonetically on the exposure sheet (x-sheet). After that comes the timing stage. At first this may sound odd, given all the references above regarding timing in relation to an animatic. Bear in mind that animatic timing is only a rough timing to set a sense of action and flow of the finished product; a sheet timer must still use the x-sheet (as discussed under the Sheet Timer topic in Chapter 5) in order to map out the timing of every step of the action, including those poses that go in-between what the animatic depicts. These x-sheets (which are a standardized and specialized form used throughout the industry) serve as the step by step guideline telling the animation house what to do. X-sheets divide into frames of animation as rows on the page, counting 24 frames and then starting over again. Using each space and going down the page, the sheet timer makes marks indicating how long each action will last, sometimes writing notes or drawing diagrams as appropriate. Again, a full description of this process lies beyond the range of this text.

Next comes the step of lip sync, which involves transcribing the letter codes that work in conjunction with the mouth charts (as discussed earlier this chapter) on to the x-sheets. As with the action, there is a specialized column on the x-sheet expressly for this purpose that corresponds with the action notes. This tells the animators how to coordinate the mouth movements of the characters with the movement of the action on-screen. Lip sync can be, but is not always, done by the same sheet timer that choreographs the action. A normal pause edit of the episode, either on cassette or on a mag track (magnetic track featuring the audio), must be provided to the person doing the lip sync.

After the lip sync person returns the slugged x-sheets, all materials go on to the checking department. They do just as the name implies, which is look over the materials and make sure that the x-sheets and storyboards all convey the same instructions. If any problems are found, corrections are made before the materials ship to the animation house.

FINAL MODEL APPROVAL

Concurrent with the timing, lip sync and checking process, the model sheets receive any final touches necessary that may have been precipitated by storyboard notes. These scenarios can range from a minor tweak in look to completely replacing the model. If possible these model changes are redrawn into the board panels before shipping but sometimes time is not on a production's side.

SHIPPING FOR PRODUCTION

Once all the materials are approved, they must be sent to the animation house. Traditionally, especially in my early experience, shipping day amounted of racing to get all the photocopies made before the international courier came, sometimes asking him to come back later that evening as things ran behind schedule. Today, with the advent of FTP to handle large file transfers, these days are almost all but gone, replaced instead with uploading to a common transfer site. Exactly how this is done, and what is transferred and what may still be shipped, varies by the budget and comfort level of each studio with technology. The items sent in the initial shipment include:

- all final black and white models pertinent to the production (e.g., specific episode of a TV show or sequence of a film, especially if multiple studios are working on the same film)

- storyboards

- x-sheets

- animatic (which also serves the studio's source of a rough audio track to animate to in most cases these days, the finished animation will often be dropped in over a transfer of the animatic)

LEAPING TO LIFE IN COLOR

After sending the black and white final model overseas, copies go to the color department where "color markups" or "color keys" are made based on a pre-agreed palette type and brand between the producers and the animation house. These color markups work with a guide to tell the animation house's paint department (generally digital these days) precisely what colors to use on each model to create the producer's desired look. Like the black and white models, the final color models (either distributed as printouts or digitally) must be approved by the producers before going to the animation house. Traditionally, color markups followed two weeks after black and white final art, but with the changing speed of production in the light of FTP and other means to share items quickly without international shipping, deadlines have fluctuated somewhat from this based on the needs and speed of the production.

SPECIAL CONSIDERATIONS

Opening Title and Music Video Design Process

Two main differences exist in the process outlined above when it comes to credit sequences and music videos. Instead of breaking down a script, the Production Coordinator breaks down the lyrics in conjunction with knowing what direction the producer wishes to take the visuals. What locations or props are suggested by the lyrics? What characters are needed for the sequence (all the main characters for credits, but can vary for music videos)? This information comprises the model breakdown list. Also, instead of a normal pause edit, a rough music recording serves as the audio basis for the process, with lip sync done to the lyrics; the final music track becomes added in post-production. Otherwise, the processes remain the same.

Dubbing Foreign Animation (ADR)

As stated in Chapter 2 ("Deciding What to Make"), only parts of this process apply to the dubbing foreign animation process. Basically this amounts to the advice relevant to casting and voice recording, based on a script written by watching the footage in conjunction with a straight translation of the plot and dialogue, and then crafting new lines that fit the plot but also the mouth movements of the existing footage. After the voices are recorded to sync in time with the existing animation, the producer of a dubbed project moves straight into post-production, as completed animation already exists. Post-Production information appears in Chapter 9.

Rotoscoping

There is a case where a detailed storyboard does not play a role in an animated production. Some directors and producers choose to let live action footage form the underlying basis of their animation, mainly for capturing fluid movements in cel animation. The name for this process is rotoscoping. A storyboard may accompany this footage, but it is more a guide than a template. Still, model sheets remain important in rotoscoping in order to keep the animation style that will be drawn over the live action footage consistent. Rotoscoping will be discussed more in Chapter 8, "Production."

A Word about the Stop-Motion Animation Process

Animation that uses the stop-motion techniques used in *Chicken Run* or the *Wallace and Gromit* films, or in television a show like Cartoon Network Adult Swim's *Robot Chicken*) is not addressed here in-depth because the process is very drastically different. Not only is the pre-production in house, but in these cases all phases of production (except possibly post) need to remain in-house due to the nature of how these projects are made. Other than possibly some beginning conceptual drawings, characters in particular are formed by continual experimentation with the actual models themselves until the right look and feel is achieved versus modeling on paper; the same applies for props. Set construction is closer to the philosophies of live-action set construction, but on a miniature scale. Consult additional resources if one's heart is set on a stop-motion animation project.

SUMMING IT ALL UP

After the script gets final approval, it then must be looked over to discover what the major characters, layouts and props are that appear in the production. While these lists are compiled and handed out to the model artists to do their work, a voice track for the project is recorded. These preliminary models and the audio then get passed out to storyboard artists who create a rough storyboard for staging that is subsequently cleaned up to make it standardized and more 'on model'; after the board clean up, these elements are edited together into an animatic (also known as a leica reel) to look for story or staging problems. As the models become finalized, they are 'pasted up' on standard sheets identifying their production number, episode (if applicable), type of model, and first scene of appearance in the production. After both animatic and models are finalized, the whole package moves on to timing and lip-sync, where character movement of body and mouths is worked out. After the checking department gives one last pass, all the black and white elements get sent to the animation house with color markups to follow.

CHAPTER EIGHT

Production

SCOPE AND FOCUS

Entire books exist on the market covering how to animate. This holds true for all major forms of animation: 2D cel, 3D CGI, and Flash. Other less common formats, such as stop-motion, are outside the scope of this particular text. This chapter aims to offer an overview of the process steps, though not necessarily details on how each step is performed. Also, it includes other areas specifically of interest to the producer, such as how key the Overseas Supervisor is in this phase of the process and how to handle situations where portions of the animation need to be re-done.

HOW 2D MODELS BECOME CEL ANIMATION

Using 2D Models and Storyboards as a Guide for Animation Drawings

When the 2D models arrive at the animation studio, they are handed out with copies of the storyboard to the various animators assigned to work on different parts of the production. The animator follows the storyboard for the action, using the 2D models as a guide to make sure the characters, props, and layouts carry the same consistent look and feel throughout the project. These drawings either capture every frame of needed movement (which is animating on "ones") or every other frame of movement (animating on "twos") as first mentioned in Chapter Four, "Financing, Scheduling, and Budgeting." The work first takes place on paper to allow for easier correction at this stage if a look is not quite right, or details must be changed; once a drawing becomes inked on a cel, it becomes more of a challenge to revise.

The only variance in this process is if the animators are provided live action footage they are asked to use as the template to base the animation on, with a process known as rotoscoping. In that case, the animators project the live action film and trace the figures frame by frame, but dress them and adapt their looks to match the model sheets provided. Again, digital equipment helps this process because a frame of the digitized live action footage can be imported into an art program and utilized within.

With animated features, sometimes the pencils are shot using a camera and edited to the audio track before work proceeds further. This version, called a pencil test, is so that any problems with animation can be caught and corrected before moving on to the ink and paint stages. Smaller studios and direct-to-DVDs are less likely to use this approach than large-budget, big-studio features.

Tracing on to the Cel

After pencils are complete, these drawings are given to inkers who then must copy the drawings to animation cels. They do this by laying the paper drawing under their animation cel and then using ink to copy the artwork. A good inker should end up with drawings that match the approved paper ones. On productions where everything happens digitally, this is easily achieved with the layer effects in art programs once pencil drawings are scanned into the computer.

Painting Cels

Cel painters use the color markups provided of the models to capture the exact color palette the producer and director want for the production. In case of error, traditional cel paint wipes clean fairly easy due to being an acrylic based paint. That said, it can dry out and begin to chip off over a long period of time. Here again, technology makes it easier to paint the cels when they are in the computer as it becomes easier to select precise colors and paint more efficiently and thoroughly.

Shooting the Finished Animation Footage

The process of shooting the finished animation footage, known traditionally as "camera," has equally changed with the times. While there are some independent animators who still shoot cels on to individual frames of film using a traditional multiplane camera, most have digitally ink and painted cels which are transferred into computer programs and assembled into their proper order based on the approved animatic or pencil test. This final digital package then must be output to a format as desired by the producer, usually some form of digital tape but sometimes to a large hard disk.

Even with animation shot to traditional film, it often will be digitized (projected in such a way that the film images are converted into a digital capture of the animation). This results in very little animation actually edited in post on film stock. Be aware that the following chapter on Post Production (Chapter 9) will reflect a digital process.

THE EVOLUTION OF 3D MODELS INTO ANIMATION

Going from 2D to 3D Models

The road map for creating any 3D model begins with the 2D model drawn and approved, as discussed in Chapter 7 ("Pre-Production"). While the 2D version will not show all possible perspectives, it does provide a blueprint for the desired look and feel of an item. The 3D artist then uses that use a 3D program (ones used professionally include *Maya, 3D Studio Max,* and *Lightwave*) to create what is called a "wireframe" structure, which looks exactly like it sounds—the shape of the object built using a gridlike structure.

Wireframes are the skeleton of each model and this stage is the most crucial. Not only does someone get the sense of an item's full shape, it provides the first opportunity to see if something structurally about that item will not work with the other elements in the animation. If something must be altered, it can be done at this stage with far less hassle and rendering time than at the later stages.

There are two levels of quality to any 3D model. The first type, low polygon models, only suggest major details and therefore take less time to render (create). High polygon models due to their higher detail require more rendering time which in turn costs more money, so they usually are reserved for the final animation stages. Figure 8.1 shows a 2D drawing of a pair of binoculars; Figure 8.2 shows that 2D drawing translated into a low polygon count 3D wireframe and a high polygon count wireframe.

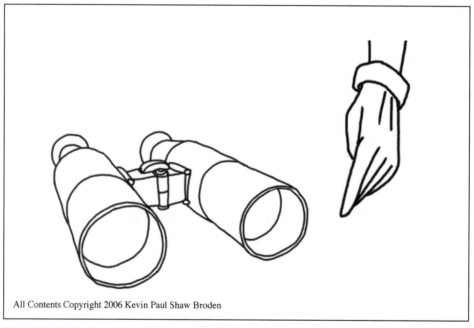

Figure 8.1 – 2D Drawing of Binoculars

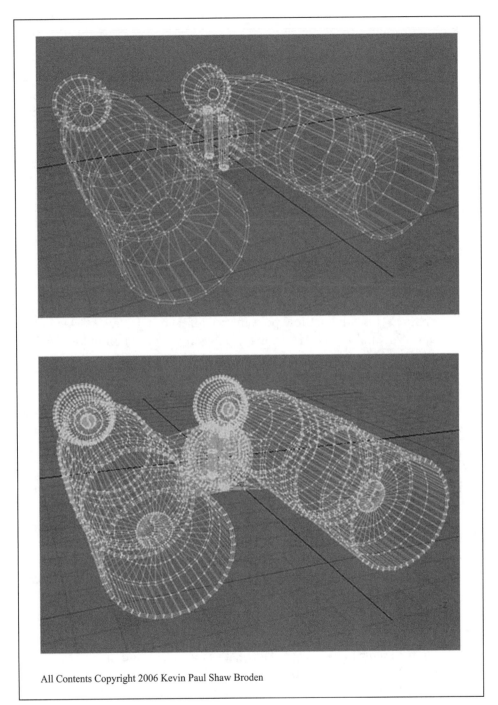

Figure 8.2 – 3D Low and High Polygon Count Wireframe of Binoculars

Texturing

Some items require special surfaces—such as prints, logos, or other distinct features. This process is called texturing. A separate texture artist creates a flat layout that will ultimately wrap around the 3D model after it receives separate approval. A specific example I can think of is a floral print pattern for a tissue box that we used in an episode of *Noddy*. The rendered box could easily have been painted flat colors, but the decision was made for a design to be placed on it. A separate 2D model of the texture was drawn and colored, and provided to the 3D animators who did the same and got that approved before placing it on the separately rendered tissue box.

From Wireframe Models to Full Rendering

With the underlying wireframe constructed, and beginning in conjunction with the textures are still being worked on and approved, the next step is to make this into a solid version of the object without the texture. This solid yet low polygon version allows for early detection of any structural issues. Also, the low polygon version of all models will be used to render a rough low resolution (also known as "lo-res") animation of the production, which is essentially a lower quality version of the final product. The purpose of the "lo-res" version is to iron out any timing, texturing, lighting or staging issues that were not apparent on the storyboard. This rough animation will be viewed and notes made upon it, for the animators to resubmit new "lo-res" versions if required until the process is refined. Think of this as a 3D animatic, in a sense.

Once the "lo-res" version gains the approval of all parties on the production, the final version (using high polygon count items) will be rendered, which will take longer to complete due to the longer render time required for the greater detail. This sometimes is referred to as a "hi-res" version, short for high resolution. Notes may still occur at this stage, usually in color and texturing, but the hope is that most issues will have been caught watching the "lo-res" version and thereby making this high polygon count version of the product immediately ready to move into post-production (See Chapter 9).

On the following two pages, Figure 8.3 shows a low and high polygon flat shaded version of the binoculars, while Figure 8.4 shows them in a textured state for both low and high polygon counts.

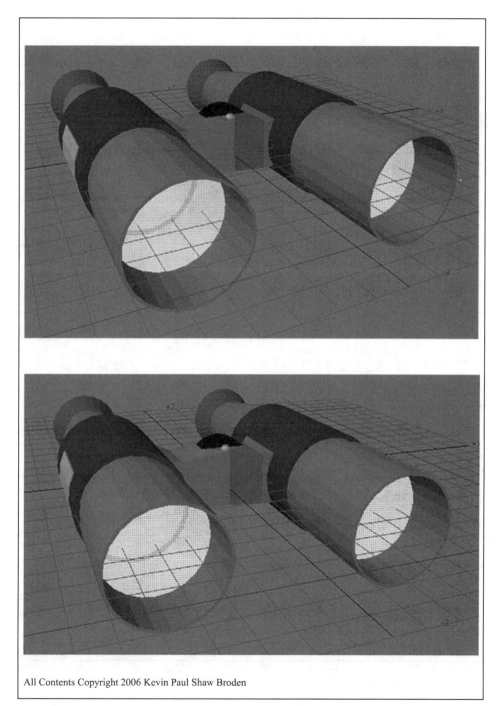

Figure 8.3 –Low and High Polygon Flat Shaded Version of Binoculars

Figure 8.4 – Low and High Polygon Textured Version of Binoculars

Gardner's Guide to Writing and Producing Animation

3D Animation and the Art of Inbetweens

3D animation offers two options for dealing with the issue of inbetweens:

Motion Capture: Motion capture involves putting human beings in specially designed suits that have sensors on every joint. These people then act out the scenes of the animation, and how they move is recorded ("captured") to then be imported into the computer and digitally interpreted using the sensors to give the same range of motion to the animated characters; in some ways, it can be seen as a digital equivalent of rotoscoping. Motion capture tends to be used more in productions where more realistic movement is desired, but can be used to advantage on any project for a higher degree of control; the downside is the cost of rental and staging of the motion capture.

Keyframes: The 3D keyframe process bears some similarities to the keyframe and inbetween process described for 2D cel animation. Basically, only the keyframes are animated, and then the computer calculates what in between motions are required to make the object or part of the object (such as a character's arm) move logically from Point A to Point B. Based on those calculations, it then computes and renders all the inbetween steps. This technique's downside is that it makes it difficult to produce realistic motion at times, and can have more of a "doll-like" effect if not done with great care and time; however, that very look may be desirable for certain properties. For example, the *Noddy* interstitials I worked on involved characters that were toys, so in this case using simple keyframe movements of the characters proved very appropriate.

Dealing with Lip Sync

Lip sync is achieved by using preset files in the 3D program of choice that tell the computer model to move its facial features to match certain positions for the various phonemes, just as in a mouth chart. The files then are used to assemble combinations that create the needed lip sync movement. Though an audio track can be imported to sync to, additional information can be obtained from x-sheets.

BRINGING FLASH ANIMATION TO LIFE

Flash animation bridges the gap halfway between cel and fully computer rendered animation. Flat characters, similar to cel drawings, are utilized but are done so in a computer environment that makes them easier to manipulate. The computer's instructions tell it to move the flat drawings by way of keyframes and then it can fill in the blanks with inbetweens to create the illusion of motion; depending on the complexity of the motion a lot of keyframes may still be needed as Flash is closer to the limitations of cel animation than the full range of motion that 3D animation can compute for. This factor tends to be the main one that makes Flash look as limited, if not more so, than "limited" cel animation which is done on "twos" (meaning every other frame is animated).

SPOTLIGHT INTERVIEW

TIM YOON

Tim Yoon's credits include work as Production Manager on *Mucha Lucha!,* a highly-rated Flash-animation series for Warner Bros. Television Animation. He has also worked as Associate Producer on *The Buzz on Maggie,* Walt Disney Television Animation's first Flash series. At the time of this writing, Tim Yoon serves as Line Producer for a Flash animation series at Nickelodeon, which has the distinction of being Nickelodeon's foray into in-house Flash animation production. He shares some of his experience working with Flash.

"Technically, Flash is 2D. It's just produced using Flash. There are many benefits, but two important benefits over a traditional production are the symbol library [since] this allows animators to efficiently reuse any drawing in the scene, and allows artists the ability to have characters with lots of details that don't need to be redrawn on every frame. The other advantage is the ability for creative retakes. In a traditional production you have animators, scanners, ink and painters, and compositors. A good Flash animator does all those roles and pretty quick.

I think one of the major setbacks is that the software is not keeping up with the animators. The majority of users are still web based and that is who Macromedia is catering to. It was great in the beginning when we were using Flash 4 for broadcast television. Now we're up to Flash 8, and it hasn't drastically improved. As far as the animation itself, that is up to the director and the animator. It can look as good or bad as they want it to look.

At the end of the day, whether you use Flash or U.S. Animation, you're still making a 2D cartoon. You need talented animators, designers, painters, storyboard artists, and writers. They just need to know different software, which is always evolving. We're all using Flash now, but what will we be using 10 years from now?"

COMMON QUESTIONS FROM ANIMATION HOUSES

To expect that a production's carefully checked and packaged materials will go off to the animation house without raising any questions at the other end is an unrealistic expectation. Whether or not a language barrier comes into play, there always will be something the animation house needs to know, though not all may actually ask the needed questions. Here are examples of what might come up:

Conflicts between the models and storyboard: The animators are asked to do something that doesn't seem possible to them. I remember going around and around on one show about a staircase that did not match between the model and the storyboard. The difference proved to be so subtle that it made it through all the pre-production phases without being caught, and then the first couple of times the animation house inquired our side of the production did not see the problem. We had to ask them in great detail why it was not usable in order to clear up the issue. Ultimately a minor modification was made and it all worked out.

Instructions not clear: This most often occurs when translators have to convert the language of the pre-production house into something the people there understand, and end up with a translation that makes no sense to them. Usually this question comes to the producer through the Overseas Supervisor, who is unable to sort out the question for the animation house.

Buying more time: A scene or set of scenes may take longer to do than expected, or so the animation house says, so they ask for more time. Evaluate each situation and scrutinize it carefully against the production schedule and how important this particular piece is to the whole. Becoming too generous with giving more time sets a bad precedent and ultimately can hamper delivery deadlines.

SPOTLIGHT INTERVIEW

JOSH PRIKRYL

Josh Prikryl began his career in the field as a 3D animator on series such as *Voltron: The Third Dimension* and *Max Steel* for the now defunct studio Netter Digital. Josh's knowledge and skills were called upon to supervise work at outsourced studios. He's since been hired by Mike Young Productions as Overseas Supervisor on series such as *Butt Ugly Martians*, *Pet Alien*, and *Bratz*. He talks about working as an overseas producer on a series.

Generally, an overseas supervisor of an animation production helps to enforce the will of the client (animation) studio, with that of the out source animation studio, overseas. One must help facilitate production and keep your bosses' studio both positive and focused, while mostly working with the client 2D director, producer, and others while you're in the confines of an overseas animation studio, far away. Basically the job is to oversee the production and help make it on-time and on-budget. Because there are strict schedules for animation shows, it is necessary to have a clear understanding about all aspects of production; from asset building, to layout, animation, lighting, rendering, compositing, and fx. One needs to be able to look at a given shot, sequence, or whole episode, and be able to determine exactly how much time it should take to produce. An overseas supervisor will juggle all aspects of production skillfully, and be able to quickly ascertain and size-up 'any situation' and solve problems quickly, including human problems, but with an appropriate prioritization to the task. An overseas supervisor needs to also understand, that in any given studio, there are competition jobs which are in conflict with ones' own production(s). There are politics in studios and it helps to be as diplomatic as possible. Moreover, one always must be willing to occasionally 'fight' for one's production, if necessary, just to ensure its survival. And you must give the constant impression that you are willing to do so. It's the ultimate mother-hen type of job—your tv show is your baby. The reality is, is that it is a multi-million dollar product which perhaps hundreds of people are counting on to 'GO RIGHT.' If it screws up, it affects hundreds of people at all levels—so there's a lot on the line and certainly not everyone is suited for this kind of responsibility or really understand the full impact of what the job entails. If the overseas animation production is like an 'out of control train,' doing something as simple as changing a production's direction can be like standing on the tracks in front of this train. And the conductors speak a foreign language half the time, with occasional attitude towards the 'spy/mother hen' in their midst. So basically, if anything goes wrong it takes a long time to change things, while often dealing with multiple people's different priorities and emergencies. A TV animation production either lives or dies by its' delivery schedules. What an overseas supervisor does not do, hopefully, is to quit. Ever.

Right now we have four (4) TV series being animated at five (5) different studios. We're about to start a fifth series, this summer. This is a little more than usual, though. In the previous six years, I personally was used to handling one, or even one and a half, long-form projects per year, maximum, allowing for much more time to devote to individual shots. Now I'm helping to manage the studios' work with broader strokes, as I'm traveling around to the various studios, throughout the month.

The bosses need confidence that a production is going as it should. Regular production reports—and projections, which are key (one must be able to predict production)—help them determine everything from payments to pre-and-post-production schedules. Rather than merely bitching to them about problems, I try & offer them specific alternative routes around problems, so they can decide what is best to do. I try giving them choices so it's both fluid and succinct. A level of professionalism and mutual respect, with a bit of daily humor thrown in—makes the flow very nice. If the show is on-time and of good quality, the flow is even better!

With experienced studios, I usually can predict, within a few days margin of error, a show's delivery—months ahead of time. I try to 'make a difference' within the playing ground of a chaotic situation in different foreign locales. Production is by definition, chaos, not unlike a construction project with all of it'd problems."

RETAKES

Types of Retakes

A "retake" is exactly as the name implies, that a scene of animation needs to be redone for some reason. Retakes break down into two major categories: technical and creative. What category a retake belongs to carries significance because it dictates who will bear the cost for that retake.

Technical retakes: These kind of retakes come about due to errors on the animation house's end that does not result from unclear or incorrect directions from the producer. These problems that need correction range from characters being painted the wrong colors, to jerky animation movements, to the wrong props being used in a scene (just to name a few examples). If a producer wishes to claim a retake as a technical one, he or she needs to be well prepared to back it up with supporting documentation clearly showing the animation house to be in the wrong. While the animation house may be more than willing to do the additional work, footing the bill for it may be another matter.

Creative retakes: Creative retakes stem from the producer wanting to make changes after seeing finished footage. Also in this category are cases where the animation house did what the materials told them to do, but the pre-production staff made a mistake in how this information was conveyed (for which the producer often takes the blame for not catching it) or gave the wrong instructions. Here, the producing company must absorb the cost of replacing the footage.

Is There Time For Retakes… And If Not, What Can Be Done?

In either case, the producer comes up against the issue of time. How quickly retakes can be turned around (sent back) depends on the number of scenes needed and the number of days until the project is due. Often, it becomes necessary to prioritize retakes into "high" and "low" categories (sometimes also a "medium" category if there are many) to try and complete the highest quality project possible. Otherwise, animation houses can easily return footage as they feel like it, without any deadline framework to adhere to.

If time does not allow for new footage to be created, the producer has a couple options. Greg Weisman illustrated one such example back in Chapter 3 ("Focusing on the Story"), where the mistake could be edited around with minimal impact to the final production. Footage from elsewhere in the production, if it can be placed in logically, may be used to substitute for the unusable footage; this solution most makes sense in situations where dialogue does not play a role or the existing dialogue can appear to be spoken "off screen" to the existing footage. If recording is done locally, it may be possible to bring actors back from the affected footage to dub new lines to correct the mistake, but odds are this will not be an option.

SUMMING IT ALL UP

This chapter walked through the process of creating both 2D and 3D animation in broad strokes. Seeing how the pipeline works, even if the Producer is not an artist, can help him or her better understand when problems arise. Being prepared to answer questions that overseas animation houses may have is crucial, and having a strong Overseas Supervisor to help bridge the gap critical. Several options exist to handle retakes—including having the animation house redo the footage, edit around the issue, reuse footage, or do ADR recording—provided time permits for correction.

CHAPTER NINE

Post-Production

RECEIVING THE RAW FOOTAGE

After an episode (or a previously agreed upon set of scenes, in a feature) are completed, the animation house returns them to the production company. At this point they are reviewed and assembled into first a "rough cut," and then, after everyone has given their approval, a "final cut" which becomes the version that will be distributed and/or exhibited. Going from raw materials to "final cut" is called post-prod-uction. There are two processes in post-production that ultimately merge together into the final edit: the video post process and the audio post process.

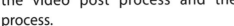

THE VIDEO POST PROCESS

Making a Work Print

The first thing needed is a work print to view the state of the footage returned from the animation house. Depending on the camera process for the footage, it could be simple as using a computer to assemble scenes onto a digital tape, or running a telecine session (basically projecting film using a single lamp with no color correction, etc.) to capture the footage shot to film to tape. This work print then receives review by the producer and all other parties to look for major errors and call for retakes if needed. The footage then proceeds to the next step.

Color Correction

Since not all scenes of an animation project are produced on exactly the same computer, despite an agreed upon color palette, there may be slight variances detected when assembling the rough footage together. Making minor adjustments to each section so that the entire project ultimately plays as a cohesive whole is called color correction, and more recently also has come to be known as color mixing. This used to be a fairly complicated and complex task, but the use of computers helps a great deal. Video Editors can even adjust color correction of retakes (footage that comes in later) on the fly to have it match up instead of undergoing a whole separate process, if need be. It also provides the ability to add some extremely basic effects, such as glowing, without additional expensive effects work.

Adding Credits

Any animation footage drawn specifically for the beginning and ending credits, in theory, should arrive before the bulk of the actual project (but this may not always be the case). In the editing bay, it is as simple as simply instructing the computer to lay the proper title cards over the video in time with the music. However, the biggest delay tends to come in finalizing the credits themselves. Usually multiple people—not just the producer—need to sign off on exactly what the title cards will read. A word processing program can be used to mock up the layout of each and every title card, showing how many names will go on each card and for what positions, and how large to make the text for each card. Getting people's names spelled properly and titles accurate is of utmost importance. Failure to do so can make people rather upset sometimes, and if one is really unfortunate, lead to really bad consequences depending on who isn't happy.

Editing to Length, Working around Problems and Dropping in Retakes

Animation productions rarely ever, in fact almost never, come in exactly to time. Generally there tends to be an overrun of footage to allow for some playing room, and the fact it is far easier to pare down something than to have to race at the last minute and add to something to bring it up to minimum required time. All that usually happens is that some extra frames are chopped off at the starting (head) and ending (tail) of scenes throughout the project, and that takes care of most of the trimming. That said, sometimes more drastic issues can occur where a project ends up far too short or far too long compared to its expectations, whether it be due to misjudging needed footage to last minute requirements to add or remove story material, as just a couple examples.

If footage must absolutely be added, the focus must be on what will strengthen the story. Additional gratuitous action sequences, unless they bring added dynamism to a scene that lacks it, risk boring the audience if they see no purpose to the action sequences. In the scenario above on the television series, we looked toward two elements regarding the added scenes. The first was what types of additions would allow the audience to better get to know the characters, which sometimes could be combined into action sequences (e.g., how characters react in a certain situation that might be funny, scary, etc.). The second involved what types of scenes might provide added backstory or information to better enrich the world of the story. If both these major points could be accomplished in the same scene, it would be all to the better... even moreso if both points happened in an action setting, as the heart of animation involves the motion of drawings.

Sometimes errors will come back in the footage for which no time for redoing the animation exists. The various alternatives for these situations mainly were discussed in Chapter 8, "Production." Generally, however, some time and budget for retakes tends to be padded into every production schedule though the length and amount varies greatly.

If time has permitted retakes of the footage, the new footage will either be delivered scene by scene as it is complete or in an entire package by episode, depending on the arrangement with the animation house. The retakes must then undergo the same process that the rest of the project did upon its arrival and then be given to the Video Editor to be dropped in to replace the bad footage. Often the retake must be cropped to length, losing footage at the start and the top of the section. Most of the time these substitutions do not affect overall time and are just a swapout, but occasionally the needed retake is longer or shorter than the initial footage. In these instances further edits must be made to add back or reduce the overall time.

If all the possible editing has been done, and the amount of time over or under is very small, a process can be resorted to called "varispeeding"— this speeds up or slows down the footage timing so that the whole project plays slightly faster or slower. However, varispeeding must be used with great care, because apply it too much and the human eye will pick up that things are not moving at their natural rates thereby destroying the overall visual appeal of a project.

Ready for the Final Mix Session

Completion of these steps prepares the video to now be matched up with the audio portion of post-production. The audio post process happens simultaneously with the video post process. In many ways, the audio post-production process mirrors the video post-production process, yet there are also some definite distinctions. The steps that follow in the next section chart audio to the same point in the post-production pipeline.

THE AUDIO POST PROCESS

Dialogue Editing and Post ADR

In Chapter 7, "Pre-Production," the assembly of the Normal Pause Edit (a compilation of best takes with a standard, or "normal," pause between each line) was discussed. Once the footage returns from the animation house, the audio post facility can better see exactly how the audio needs to be used in relation to the picture and adjust as needed. The first step is editing the normal pause edit so that it matches the finished animation; remember that the timing of the footage came not from the Normal Pause Edit, but rather the work of the timers using the exposure sheets as also discussed in Chapter 7, "Pre-Production."

Dialogue editing, however, consists of much more than just matching sound to picture. To a degree, it also includes a first pass as other dialogue edits, such as wallas and dropping in any retakes that may not have been sent to the animation house (as can happen in cases when a dialogue retake does not influence animation, such as a line delivered when the character is off screen or has his or her back to the camera). Also, basic sweetening, such as adding additional "oohs" and "aahs" that may not have been recorded during the session but are needed to enhance the production, may be added if these sounds already exist in the dialogue library. When it comes to animation originally made in one country and dubbed into another language by a producer, dialogue is edited to picture one line at a time. This ensures each line fits where it is intended to go. The reason this is crucial is because of how important it is to try and match the lip sync as accurately as possible. In all cases, the finished dialogue track, originally edited to picture, but separate of the picture, must be "laid back" to be put in sync with the video.

As previously indicated, ADR (Automatic Dialogue Replacement) to finished originally produced animation occurs only in rare cases. For some shows like prime time animation that wish to be more topical as of first airdate it is built into the budget, but for most to use ADR is more of a last resort (such as repairing something that Standards & Practices failed to catch until the eleventh hour). This is different than in the case of producing animation in one language and dubbing it into another language, this stage is taken care of at the pre-production phase and the dialogue need only be matched to the mouths at the dialogue editing phase. Other cases include when a temporary voice track has been laid in because the actor cast for the role is not available until post-production, or a last minute recast of actors.

Sound Effects and Foley

Sound effects and Foley are related areas. Sound effects are dropped into a production by sound effects editors who have a library of sounds (usually stored digitally) to choose from; these tend to be for background noise and there is not a concern of sync (matching up to) the picture. However, there are some sound effects elements such as footsteps that must naturally match to the animated character's movements, or sounds that the sound effects editors do not have on file; this is where foley comes in.

Using a sound stage where they watch the edited picture with no soundtrack, foley artists use items that create the needed sounds to bring the picture to life. These can be anything from footsteps with a certain kind of shoe, to shaking tin foil for rain, to far more complicated maneuvers as wild and varied as the medium of animation. The sound effects editor then makes sure the foley artists' recordings become incorporated properly into the effects track.

Music Edited to Picture

Ideally, a producer communicates with the composer beginning in the pre-production stage; this especially holds true for songs that require lyrics such as a theme song. Storyboards and other visuals may be provided to give a composer the feel of a show. However, as a show goes along, incidental background music needs to be composed to underscore dramatic or comedic moments. Composers should be provided an animatic to give them a head start for the feel of the story flow and important points, but sometimes due to tight deadlines it may not be until the final footage returns from the animation house that the composer sees any moving visual picture. It is strongly recommended to bring the composer in as soon as possible to allow maximum time for creative collaboration and changes. These cues, once approved, are sent to the music editor who drops them in where directed.

Eventually, if enough cues are accumulated, the bulk of the work falls simply to the music editor. He or she selects the most appropriate piece from the library of previous cues to cover the needed impact.

SPOTLIGHT INTERVIEW

BILL KOEPNICK

Bill Koepnick is CEO of Advantage Audio, which he also co-owns with James (Jim) Hodson. Bill's 30+ years of experience as a musician, recording engineer, and sound designer helped him build the foundation of this long running company; he has done mixing and sound editing for hundreds of episodes of televised animation, and also has personally received three Emmy® Awards for Sound Editing, two Emmy Awards for Sound Mixing, and three M.P.S.E. Golden Reels for Sound Editing. One thing distinct about Advantage Audio's business is that the company built its reputation handling the post-production audio needs of animation. The company's services have been called upon by large studios and small productions alike. Advantage Audio is a full service company, from dialogue editing, to foley, to effects, and more. He shares some insight on the animation business and the role of a producer.

"We officially incorporated in 1989 and opened Advantage Audio in 1990. For pre-production we record dialog (the first step), and assemble elements (normal pause and slug to storyboards). When the picture is ready we do a full post job; recording additional dialog (and ADR), re-syncing dialog to picture, creating and editing sound effects, recording Foley, editing music (recorded elsewhere), and performing the final mix in one of our three 5.1 surround stages. Generally, we receive locked picture—or at least a video workprint that will only be revised with insert edits for minor changes to scenes that won't usually change the overall length of the episode. The video house is chosen by the production company (if they don't assemble the picture in-house), and once we have our workprint there is usually not much interaction with the video folks unless a problem arises. The producers step in if necessary to remedy any troubling issues, but those are rare occurrences.

The best producers know what they want, and are good at communicating those wants to the editors and mixers working on their project. With today's tight budgets, and time equating to money, better communication means less time and money are wasted. Organization is also critically important. Waiting for the music to be delivered on the day of the mix is a common logistical mistake. So is a failure to provide the same workprint to the composer that they gave to us. The most organized clients allow us to concentrate fully on the creative issues and not force us to worry about finding needed materials or making last-minute editorial changes to our sound elements. Producers who understand some of the technical aspects of the process are also better equipped to interact with us more effectively.

A wise producer should make a production schedule and stick to it—or be ready to find more time and/or money when the final deadline looms. As a rule it is more cost-effective to get it right from the beginning, and allow time for things to go wrong along the way. Trying to unrealistically compress the whole process into a minimum time frame and hoping all things will fall into place is a recipe for disaster. It never works that way."

THE MERGING OF THE VIDEO AND AUDIO POST PROCESS

Finally, the video and audio are brought together in a mix session. Here, all the elements are synchronized together. However, it is important to note that the dialogue becomes placed on one audio track of the finished production, while music and effects (also called M&E for short) end up mixed onto another track. This is so that when and if other countries purchase the rights to dub a producer's animation into that country's native language, all they need to do is replace the dialogue track and leave the remaining elements intact.

In some studios, this process occurs with the producer in the studio. In others, the first mix to video will be done to a time coded tape and then the producer will give notes on what needs changing and a second mix will be done; this usually occurs when the producer cannot be right there in the session to make the desired tweaks in person. In both cases, a couple of passes are required to lock everything down.

CLOSED CAPTIONING AND ALTERNATE DIALOGUE TRACKS

When it comes to animated television episodes, there is an additional step. While this process takes place, an "as aired" version of the script (in particular, containing all the finalized lines of dialogue) must be completed. This "as aired" script is sent with a copy of the first pass at a tape containing dialogue, music, and effects to a closed captioning facility that does the special process of translating the script to closed captioning format. This information is provided on a special kind of storage device that is then returned to the post-production house and laid on a track of the finished production. Second audio tracks (such as the SAP, or Spanish language audio track found on some programs in the United States) are also embedded the same way.

GETTING READY FOR DELIVERY

Cue Sheets

Cue sheets are forms listing all the music used in a production, particularly those covered by ASCAP, BMI, or SESAC in the United States and other music societies throughout the world. Their primary purpose is to report back to the various societies about the use of the materials so the composers are appropriately compensated. Cue sheets also serve as a document of all music (cues and full songs) in a specific production, what order they appear in, and the duration of each piece of music. Depending on the situation, the production company submits these directly or the production company sends them to the distributor who then forwards them to the societies. In the case of the *Noddy* interstitials, I received the cue information from our music editor and placed it into sheets provided by PBS; I then forwarded the sheets to the Director of Copyright at PBS to then be forwarded to the societies.

Dubs and Deliveries

After the final editing session, copies must be made to be sent to everyone agreeing to distribute or exhibit the project. This can be done either via satellite (where the distributors take responsibility for collecting the feed on their end) or onto a physical form of media for delivery referred to as dubs. Dub copies may be all the same format (digital tape, film, etc.) or spread out among multiple formats dependent upon the distribution agreement. After that, the production company must arrange to have the finished versions delivered to the distributors, either via courier in local cases or carrier (such as UPS, FedEx, DHL or other carriers) outside the local area. Preferred carriers will usually be specified by each distributor and exhibitor.

SUMMING IT ALL UP

A work print is created when the raw footage returns from overseas as the first step in the video post process, followed by color correction. Credits must be assembled, approved, and prepared, along with any title sequences. After all the elements are ready, the animated project will be edited to length—sometimes working around problems and dropping in retakes in the process. The audio post work starts with dialogue editing and any required ADR work, as well as dropping in sound effects, creating foley effects, and editing music to picture. For television episodes, after video and audio are mixed together (including a second language audio track if required), the tape goes along with an "as aired" script to add closed captioning text which is embedded into one of the media tracks. Cue sheets, detailing all the music in the production, are prepared to ultimately be delivered to the societies that represent the music composers. After these steps are completed, the finished product will either be copied and sent to the relevant distributors or sent out via satellite for the exhibitors to record.

PART FOUR:
Getting Your Animated Product Out There

CHAPTER TEN

The Art of Distribution, Exhibition, and Marketing

THE "FINAL CUT" IS READY TO BE SHOWN

At last, all the hard work seems to be behind the producer, with a project completed and ready to be shown (feature film, television pilot, or short). However, in the eyes of some, the hard work really begins now. Unless the producer is on a work-for-hire, or commenced production with a distribution or exhibition guarantee as part of the pipeline, now the producer must convince someone else to take the risk to make the finished production commercially accessible for a large number of other people to experience. The focus of this chapter applies to those brave souls who create a project without knowing how or where the public will get to see it, and what their options are.

The first steps to getting that distribution or exhibition involves getting the finished product in the hands of people who can make it happen. There are a couple ways to do this.

Festivals

Many executives attend film festivals looking for new product and talent. Some festivals specialize in animation, while others are broader in base. What matters here is that a producer fit in festivals with a similar theme where the piece will fit in yet not blend in; being part of an exhibition that is not a fit may call more attention to the piece in an unintended negative way.

Showing a Finished Project to Executives

Sometimes, instead of hoping executives will be scouting festivals to come to a producer, the producer may find it more advantageous to bring the finished project (or a sampler of it) to those who can distribute or exhibit it. While some companies have open door policies for unsolicited material, bear in mind that many require receiving it through some form of representation (such as an attorney, agent, or manager).

Digital Distribution

This would cover distribution websites (versus just having a webpage advertising the project's availability) and downloads such as video-equipped MP3 players. Unless a producer can afford a company's own server, this may still require working with a distribution partner; some may be open to anything, while others are more restrictive in their content. As technology changes rapidly, this could become a more feasible option for many projects and make it easier to reach more specialized audiences initially to work toward a wider release.

SPOTLIGHT INTERVIEW

JERRY BECK

Jerry Beck is well known for his involvement in several facets of animation. Known by many as an animation historian, Jerry's also worked organizing animation festivals and at one time even worked as an animation development executive. Most recently, he's produced the short *Hornswiggle* with G7 Animation for Frederator's *Random Cartoon* series for Nickelodeon. He gives would-be producers some advice on breaking into the industry.

"If you have a completed animated short film, there are several advantages. You can enter it in festivals and hopefully gain exposure, audience acceptance and win awards. Network scouts could see the reaction and decide to want to option the film or the property from you. Beavis & Butt-head started this way. Commercial Festivals like *The Animation Show* or *Spike & Mike* may pay you to use your film in theatrical showings. You could license the film for use to several cable channels as 'filler.' Personal Video players are new sources of revenue for a short film maker. Exposure on the internet can also raise attention for your short and your ideas. Having a finished film shows the networks what you can do. It's a great calling card. But you could pitch four or five other ideas in the time it takes to make such a film. You may never get back the money/time you invest in such an effort. That is your big risk. But if you have a good idea—it's worth it.

An alternative to festivals is pitching a finished pilot directly to the studios and networks. You have two choices. Send the finished film into a network exec… and wait. Or make an appointment, pitch the concept in person, screen a few minutes with the exec—and leave the DVD with them to consider it and show it to their bosses. I'd suggest the latter method. In person contact is much more important. The exec wants to see the person behind the project. If it sells, you will be working together—they want to feel comfortable with you.

There is no such thing as a 'bad meeting' in Hollywood. No one wants to have a bad experience. Network execs WANT to like your project… but it has to fill a particular need or network agenda to be considered seriously. So take a meeting, and don't expect a 'yes' or 'no' in the meeting. They'll get back to you—or you'll follow up in a week. It's important to meet the people you want to sell to. Never discuss 'merchandising' with network execs. Always be positive and enthusiastic. Don't pitch anything you don't totally love. Don't try to guess what they are looking for. Create something you really want to see on television."

LESS TRADITIONAL OPTIONS FOR MARKETING

One of the nice things about getting tied into a festival is that it helps take care of the marketing aspects for the showings of the animated project (since the project will be showcased as one of the festival offerings). However, if a producer needs to let people know the finished property is available of which they might not otherwise be aware, there are a few options available besides just the traditional posters, flyers, and postcards that come to mind.

The Internet

A producer might invest in a webpage with information about the finished product and how to contact the producer. If it can be afforded, sample clips might even be available. However, a producer should use restraint and not give away too much of the plot or business information upfront; the goal is to intrigue potential partners, and not come off looking too demanding.

Online Chat and Comment rooms

The producer builds a rapport with people that have interests similar to the film. After they get to know him or her (not on the first visit to the room, or it will be interpreted simply as an ad), the producer can then tell about the project and see who knows anyone that may be interested or if enough interest can be generated to gather all these interested people to approach a potential partner showing a possible audience. Overall, this approach should be viewed as a very risky one and to only be used if a producer has built a true rapport with a specific online community; if a producer does not come off as genuine, no one has any reason to take the self-promotion seriously. Frankly, it's better if others can do this kind of word of mouth advertising for the producer so it looks a little less egotistical, but still it must be approached with discretion.

Conventions

These are the same conventions mentioned in Chapter Four ("Financing, Budgeting, and Scheduling") that tend to cater to buyers, or other media conventions that cater more to the public but have strong followings (such as Comic-Con International: San Diego). Some of these conventions have their own showings a producer might be able to become a part of, but even if not, a producer should always attend with a one-page information of information in hand ready to hand out to anyone who may show serious interest. Even without flyers, conventions are still a great opportunity for word of mouth buzz.

Gimmick Promotional Mailings

This is still done as a form of mass mailing to potential investors, trying to use some unique hook or angle to be noticed (such as specially shaped flyers, or cookies, or other things) but is strongly going out of favor based on what I have heard from others and seen in my own personal entertainment industry experiences when I have done temporary work outside of animation (such as in production companies with casting divisions). Not only does it tend to be overdone, when taking into consideration today's heightened mail security in places like the United States, a too-inventive package might raise some eyebrows and never make it to the recipient. Still that doesn't stop some people from trying. The same rules go for a mass emailing; many people's programs will see the large number of recipients and immediately flag the content as spam, which means a high likelihood the content will never be read.

Overall, marketing is a challenging business. What works to market one property may not work for another.

SPOTLIGHT INTERVIEW

JAN NAGEL

Jan Nagel worked for advertising agencies for half of her career and then fell into VFX and animation in 1991 when the ad agencies were going through a really bad time; she's stayed in the animation business ever since. Since 2002 Jan has worked independently, representing animation studios and creators. She represents international production studios and creators of animation, helping them realize their personal goals, like getting production work or selling a show. She offers some insight into what studios are looking for and how make it as a producer.

"Frankly, it is wiser not to produce the final project until one have pitched the concept around first. If you don't get any interest and one have the funds, go and make the film, but know that your return of investment for a short subject is limited. Do it because it is your way of proving your talent. The first thing any producer needs to take into consideration is what the target audience for their film is. Producers make the mistake of saying their film is for 'all audiences'. This is way too broad. Is it an animation for children, teens or adults? Is it for boys or girls? Is this an art film that the producer is doing for their soul, or is it a film that they want to showcase their talent and launch their commercial career? This will help determine the various venues for display.

In the past, short films or one-off films were limited in where they could be shown and there are very few distributors that handle short films. If the film is an art piece or a work to launch a career it could be headed for the festival circuit where distributors are looking for the best that will fit into their libraries. However, today, networks, like Nicktoons and Cartoon Network look for shorts as an incubator to future series. They use these shorts to measure audience acceptance. If there is an interested audience then it might go into series development. One such show is *Chalk Zone* which was part of the *Oh Yeah! Cartoon* block and then went to series. Because there are so many new media outlets, producers need to keep their options open. Frederator, Warner Bros. and others are looking for shorts to run on the web, as iPod downloads and for Video on Demand.

If a producer goes through the expense of displaying their own film, it should be for the purpose of Oscar® consideration. There are selected festivals that the Academy of Motion Pictures Arts and Sciences will recognize and it would be far better for a film maker to put their money and effort to get into festivals and be juried, then to pay for a screening. Why, because distributors attend festivals, as well as network executives, looking for the next big hit.

As a marketing professional, I look at the property and ask the questions about purpose and audience. Then I create a strategic plan of promotion. This plan might be to identify specific distributors, networks and other outlets to pitch the completed project. Or it might be deciding a festival circuit is the way to get the best results. Either way, it is based on the project and the film maker's goals.

In the blockbuster and big box office productions whatever it costs to make a film should equal the cost of promoting the film. So a $100 million production budget should be matched with almost $100 million in prints, promotion, cross promotion, and advertising. For lower budget films, promotional dollars are needed, and sometimes a producer will cut a deal with a huge distributor like Buena Vista with the agreement that Buena Vista will not only get 35% of the box office, but the producer will supply the distributor the advertising budget. This could be risky for the producer.

The first rule in Hollywood is to never use your own money to produce your film. There are those that have taken the gamble and succeeded, but there are so many more that haven't. Before spending one dollar of your own to run the camera, put the money into a really excellent pitch and take it to distributors, networks, potential production partners, and even financiers. Get them to like the project enough to invest their skills, money, and efforts."

DEAL-MAKERS AND DEAL BREAKERS

The possibility definitely exists that a distributor or exhibitor may be eager and willing to distribute a project… if one just changes a couple of things. The reasons behind this vary so widely—from the highly logical to the extremely political—that it is tough to list them all. A common one is that it will be fear of offending their target audience (more specifically, in television, this will be the "Standards and Practices" department, while film may just depend on the specific distributor or exhibitor's guidelines). Ultimately, the producer and those who also have influential say on the project must make the call as to whether these compromises will not compromise the greater vision of the project, or if doing what is asked undercuts the project and thereby does not make an distribution or exhibition deal worth pursuing.

COPYRIGHTS AND CLEARANCES

In a studio or co-financing system, getting all of this taken care of may be pre-arranged for a producer as part of the process, and if issues arise one may be informed. If one is doing the entire project on your own, in theory your attorney that a producer selected as part of the team (see Chapter 5) should be on this the whole way so that one doesn't run into a clearance issue being a sticking point as to why a distributor won't take a project on (i.e., fear of a lawsuit); what is nice is that this kind of research will also alert a producer to potential problems and give an opportunity to ignore or correct those notes. However, a producer should not forget to double (or maybe even triple) check all this research before approaching the distributors and marketers.

DEALING WITH FEEDBACK ONCE THE PROJECT GOES PUBLIC

After all the hard work of the producer and the team, and finding a distributor or exhibitor willing to get it out there, the animation project makes its debut to the outside world. With that exposure comes people offering their thoughts on the projects, perhaps wanted or perhaps not. A producer needs to figure out how to sift through this feedback, use it when it can be constructive, and deal with it when it is of little use (either as off-base criticism or something beyond the producer's ability to correct). Criticism may still be constructive if the setting of the showing is for that purpose, such as a rough cut or a pre-release showing (at times there are stories of live action movies getting entire ending rewritten due to test audience reaction, but time and money make this less likely in animation unless the adjustment is minor). Generally, once an animated project gets shown to audience outside the production, it is considered a "locked" picture that cannot be changed.

Here are some things to bear in mind about feedback:

Try not to take it too personally: This may be easier said than done for a producer who has invested not only financially but heart and soul in a production.

Pay attention to patterns: Even though a comment someone makes may seem like something a producer disagrees with, and especially doesn't find it constructive to hear if the picture is "locked," it is worth nothing if several people make the same observation. This may reveal that something in the production could have been looked at a different way, and be something worth noting for the future. If a producer does not let people at least speak their mind, an opportunity may be missed to learn.

Be cautious of completely gushing praise: If someone gives a producer nothing but glowing feedback, particularly strong glowing comments, do not be afraid to scrutinize this person for other motives. While this person may have completely enjoyed the production, the business also intends to encourage people who want to get in "closer" to others in any way possible, as it is the downside of networking (as discussed earlier this chapter). However, if many people give positive comments on the same elements, a producer should feel confident of the job he or she—along with the crew—has done.

SUMMING IT ALL UP

Festivals, direct submission to executives, or digital distribution are the three main venues for getting people interested in a final product that doesn't already have a built in wide distribution base. Marketing is very much word of mouth in these situations, with the Internet as a showcase outlet, online chat rooms, and attending conventions as ways to spread the word; gimmicky marketing mailings are discouraged. Bear in mind a potential distributor or exhibitor may ask for revisions before being willing to take on an animated project, and the producer may have to decide whether or not these changes compromise the artistic vision and if they are worth doing for distribution. Copyrights and clearances must be checked before any piece goes public, to avoid any awkward situations legally for producer or the distributor. The producer must also become good at taking feedback, whether or not it can be incorporated into the film at this stage.

CHAPTER ELEVEN

But What Happens
After the Production's Done?

CLOSING IT ALL DOWN

Now the Show is Over

The production can end in two major ways: the completion of the animated project or closing down the production at some stage (as covered in any of the prior chapters) due to a lack of finances or other business reasons. In the case of a production not seeing the finished light of day, be prepared for it to be emotionally draining on all levels of the crew and not just the producer so use discretion and make sure all arrangements (final paychecks, etc.) are clearly known before communicating to the staff. What this chapter describes generally applies in either scenario with the exception of a couple areas, but hopefully will be used due to a happy ending.

Archiving the Production

It creeps up on a producer before he or she realizes it—the production comes to a close and the question arises of what to do with all the finished pre-production materials. The copies of the models, storyboards, normal pause edits, and the like cannot just be disposed of, especially if the producer hopes for sequel or spinoff projects. This is because saving these items may save money later on so that items do not need to be re-created. Also, with the demand for items such as DVD extras and other types of special content, there is no telling what might be needed or when.

In the case of a co-production, a production partner may specify how the materials are to be stored and for how long. It could be a matter of shipping everything to that co-producer's offices, or being responsible for storage locally. In addition, animation houses contractually need to return items to the producer as well. In the case of a 3D CGI show, for example, all items created from the 2D model references must be returned via electronic storage to the producer to be archived and potentially used in the future; the animation house as a contracted entity has no legal rights to any of the items used in the production.

More and more material simply becomes stored digitally as the whole process uses less and less paper. Depending on the project, storage may be simply finding server space. Alternatively, if much of the work took place on paper (even if these elements later were scanned for electronic transmission), renting a physical storage facility may be in order. How much space is needed varies by the size of the project, and how much of it can be stored digitally. This also is a cost the producer incurs as a long-term operating expense, running months or years after the end of actual production.

A filing system also needs to be designed to allow for easy location of the assets if something needs to be found at a later time. In the case of all-digital storage, this system would be a directory structure and file name conventions that can easily be interpreted. For boxed storage, whatever code system is designed must allow for easy identification of the contents (at least on a general level) without having to open every box.

A COMPLETED PRODUCTION'S SENSE OF CLOSURE AND ACHIEVEMENT

The "Wrap Party"... or Other Mementos

After the successful completion of a project, a crew is often rewarded by some kind of "wrap party"—in other words, a celebration that all their hard work finally comes to a close. However, such a party may be beyond the producer's budget. Regardless, some sort of memento, no matter how small, often will be given to members of the crew whether or not there is a "wrap party." Since a producer never knows who will be on his or her team in the future, it is always good to be mindful that everyone is treated professionally and with courtesy.

There are no hard and fast rules to what a "wrap party" should be, if a producer chooses to throw one for a crew. In fact, if possible, it should be customized to what can be afforded, what best fits the crew's personalities and the level of work atmosphere to which the group has worked throughout the production. This allows for anything from a dinner at a restaurant to a beach party and beyond.

Honors

Festival Awards: If a festival turned out to be how an animated project found initial exposure, these kind of awards would be given at that time. The benefits of festival awards come in getting noticed by people able to give the animation wider distribution or exhibition, and can also be mentioned in marketing the piece when taken to the masses. Festival awards most often are juried awards given to the piece as a whole.

Industry Recognition: These awards tend to come after a piece gains wider distribution than its initial distribution or exhibition, but not always. Industry awards can be given to the production as a whole or to specific individuals for their achievements on an animated project. Any of these types of recognition can be used to increase the awareness of a film or television series. This can result in encouraging extending a project's exhibition life, or in the case of television seeing a renewal for a subsequent season, but none of this is guaranteed.

THE LIFE OF THE PRODUCER AFTER A PROJECT IS OVER

Sharing Experiences

One thing a producer can do if he or she can find a venue interested to work with that producer is to share experiences. This can vary from teaching an entire course to a workshop, or even a career counseling setting working one on one as a mentor to a youth or adult.

SPOTLIGHT INTERVIEW

BROOKS WACHTEL

In addition to his teaching experience, Brooks Wachtel holds extensive credits as a writer/director/producer (and also happens to be a performing magician). His credits include shows as diverse as Fox's live-action *Young Hercules* to Saturday morning animated action shows, such as *Static Shock, Spider-Man, X-Men, The Avengers, Gargoyles: The Goliath Chronicles, Transformers: Beast Machines* to the prime time series *The Legend of Prince Valiant,* to PBS' acclaimed series *Liberty's Kids.* For younger viewers, he has penned many episodes of the pre-school hits like *Clifford the Big Red Dog* and *Rainbow Fish.* An episode Brooks wrote of *Tutenstein* won an Emmy® award in 2004, and, with his frequent co-writer Cynthia Harrison, was Emmy® nominated for an episode of *ToddWorld* in 2006. Brooks also has experience in features. He scripted the animated feature film *Twin Princes,* an American-Korean underwater *Lord of the Rings* style epic. His live-action features include *Goddess of Death,* which he also directed. In addition to his dramatic credits, Brooks Wachtel has written and/or produced many documentaries for The History Channel. With his documentary partner Cynthia Harrison, they wrote two episodes of the series, *Guarding America: The Air Force/National Guard* and *The Coast Guard.* He has also written for *The Great Ships, Search and Rescue, The Royal Navy* and *Fly Past,* the latter of which won the coveted "Cine Golden Eagle Award."

Most recently, Brooks and Cynthia work as Co-Executive Producers, co-creators—and occasionally co-writers—for the documentary series *DogFights;* originally based on a two-hour special, this documentary series for The History Channel features extensive use of photo-real CGI animation (done by their producing partner Jason McKinley) to recreate dogfights ranging from World War I to Vietnam, as often described step by step by actual pilots of the era. He shares some advice on mentoring.

"I've been lecturing one way or another since I gave a film history summary while a student at Hollywood High School. I've been a speaker at several colleges and university classes on subjects relating to film production and writing. I taught a pre-production class at Triangle Video and spoke at an honors English class at Cal State LA on fiction writing. Interaction with dull young minds. I was also disturbed by the narrow frame of reference that I found in many students. I used *Casablanca* as an example and was faced with blank confused stares. Cultural knowledge should not be so constrained by generations.

I don't know if mentoring has helped showcase my work or myself professionally. But it's been rewarding in so many other ways. On one level, I get to help—or try to help—others and that's always satisfying. Also, teaching and mentoring forces you to take a good look at yourself and your work, and, we all hope, enrich and understand yourself by the view. Teaching turned out to be not only delightful, but, cliché as it is, I think I learned more than my students.

It is also important to give back to the business (and life in general). It's always wise to remember that the student of today can be your boss tomorrow."

ONCE A PRODUCER, ALWAYS A PRODUCER?

Once is Enough, Thank You

Maybe a producer's one pet dream project became a reality. Another possibility is that the producer discovers he or she just does not have the time or energy to complete another animated project. The reality is that not everyone is cut out to be an animation producer for the long term.

Doing it All Again

Having said that, other producers may feel a total thrill and excitement working on an animation project and cannot wait to jump into the next one offered. If being an animation producer is "in the blood," stay open to opportunities that may come up. Revisit the same festivals and seminars attended to find concepts (see Chapter 2, "Deciding What to Make") or the ones gone to in search of financing and co-partners (see Chapter 4, "Financing, Budgeting, and Scheduling"). The goal should be either discovery of a new concept or networking to see who needs a producer as part of their staff of an upcoming project.

SUMMING IT ALL UP

Regardless of a decision, the producer has survived the process and should be congratulated for effort. On an animation project, or for that matter any entertainment project, things rarely are smooth. It is tough to see something all the way through, especially when things don't always go right. Even if an animation project doesn't make it to the end, it must be remembered that any experience is valuable if one is willing to learn from it.

AFTERWORD

I hope that readers gained valuable insight during this journey through the animation process. My approach in putting this book together involved trying to create what I wished would have been available to me when I started in the business years ago. I also thought of my various mentors and the wisdom I gained from their detailed assistance and the courteous giving of their time. Hopefully that same kind of love and care shine through here.

Most of all though, as this book began to take shape, I came to realize that though the role of producer serves as the guide, it feels as this book turned out to be a group story about everyone involved in the animation process —how valuable each is to the rest, parts of the whole. I think that teamwork, of passionate animation artists and non-artists, is what makes good projects happen.

Maybe I'll be saying that about yours someday.

Shannon Muir
Los Angeles, CA
August 2006

GLOSSARY

NUMERICS

2D animation – the use of flat images (such as *cels* or *Flash animation*) to create moving pictures

3D animation – the use of *CGI* to create moving pictures

A

ADR – Short for Automatic Dialogue Replacement, the process of *dubbing* dialogue

animated – pictures which are moving (see also *animation*)

animatic – a video created by combining scanned *storyboard panels* with the *normal pause edit* (also known as a *leica reel* at some companies)

animation – the art of moving pictures, for which methods include *2D animation, 3D animation, Flash animation,* and *Stop-Motion animation*

assistant – an introductory level of employment on an animation *production*, most commonly either as a *production, post-production,* or *writer* assistant

archiving – the process of storing *production elements* following the completion of a project

B

background – where events in the project take place (see also *layout* or *location*)

bible – the reference book for *writers* detailing the *concept, characters,* and *locations* for the animated series or feature

breakdown – a list detailing the *characters, layouts, props, special pose or costumes,* and *effects* used in an *episode* of an animated *series* or a *feature*

budgeting – the process of figuring out how much money can be spent on an *animated project*

business affairs – the area of a *project* that deals with *contracts, clearances,* etc. (see also *legal*)

C

casting – the process of selecting *voice actors*

cel – drawings that are created onto individual sheets of plastic and then shot one by one under a *multiplane camera* to create the illusion of motion (see also *2D animation*)

CGI – short for Computer Graphic Images (see also *3D animation*)

character – a fictional individual (not necessarily human) who takes part in the *story* of an *animated project*

checker – someone who looks over the *models, exposure sheets* and *storyboards* to ensure that they all are without errors before *shipping* them to the *animation house*

circle take – the preferred *reading* of *dialogue* by a *voice actor*

clean-up – the process of refining and correcting *production elements* (such as a *storyboard*) so that they become *final* and ready for *production* use

clearance – receiving approval from the *business affairs* or *legal* department working on a *project* that there are no problems using a specific name, place, etc.

closed captioning – the process of adding text to a *project,* designed to be read by the hearing impaired, that can only be seen using specific controls on a television set or other device used to translate the special code

color correction or **color mixing** – the process of making sure all of the *animation footage* maintains a consistent look and feel

color key – a guide as to how to paint a specific *animation element* (see also *color mark-up*)

color mark-up – a guide as to how to paint a specific *animation element* (see also *color key*)

colorist – an individual who does a *color key* or *color mark-up* of *models* to show *animators* how to apply a palette to the *cels*

composer – the person who creates the music for a *project*

concept – the genesis around which the *story* idea of an *animated project* is based

contract – an agreement, usually written but sometimes verbal, defining how two or more people will work with one another (such as in employment or on a *co-production*)

convention – sometimes referred to as a "con" for short; describes a gathering of people with similar interests and purpose

co-production – two or more *production* companies working together on an *animated project*

copyright – the claim as to who owns the legal *rights* to a particular work

credits – a listing of all individuals who worked on a *production;* some (such as *producer, director, writer*) appear at the beginning of a *film* or *television episode,* but most of them at the end

D

daytime – in contrast to *prime-time,* this term generally is used to describe animation generally geared more to either a kids or all-ages audience

delivery date – deadline by which a *project* must be turned in to the company providing the *distribution* or *exhibition*

demographics – the group of people a *project* hopes to reach (see *target audience*)

director – Individuals providing specialized creative oversight on various aspects of a *project;* examples include a voice director, *casting* director, or *animation director*

distribution – the process by which an animation project gets to people interested in seeing it

dubbing – the process of replacing one voice actor with another (see also *ADR*)

E

editor – (examples include *dialogue, animatic, story* and *video* editors)

effects – enhancements (either video or audio) to help a project seem more "real"

elements – the individual materials that make up an *animated project* (including *models, x-sheets,* etc.)

episode – a *series* of *animation projects* (usually for *television*) that usually share a consistent set of *characters* and *locations*

executive – a title indicating a level of seniority, either as a *producer* or as a general term for a high ranking person at a *network*

exhibition – the showing of an *animated film* to a group of people at once, usually at a *theater* or as part of a *festival*

exposure sheets – guides that define the frame by frame actions of a *character's* movement or speech; *mouth charts* are used to provide the "code" for a *character's* individual speech pattern in the *lip sync* part of the process

expressions – drawings of a *character* illustrating how he or she would look or react to certain situations

F

feature – a long form *film,* usually 70 minutes or more in length

festival – a specific kind of *exhibition* geared to giving exposure to certain themed *films,* or designed to give added promotion to *films*

film – compared to an *episode,* usually a stand alone story (though sometime there are *sequels*)

film stock – what *animation frames* are captured on when shot with a *multiplane camera*

final – not requiring any further approval from *producers* or *executives*

financiers – people who put up the money for making an *animated project*

Flash animation – a *2D animation* process utilizing a computer and taking advantage of *vectorization* to simplify the process

foley – the use of objects to create ambient sounds for an audio track of an *animated project*

footage – a collective term for completed *animation*

fps – *frames* per Second. Animation generally is shot at 24 *frames* per second, the standard rate for *film.* When it is transferred for *television* broadcast, frames are occasionally repeated to change the rate to 30 *frames* per second (NTSC; North American standard) or 25 *frames* per second (PAL; British standard)

frame – a single shot of completed *animation* captured to *film stock* or *video*

freelance – in comparison to *staff,* someone who contributes to the *project* but not on company payroll

FTP – File Transfer Protocol; basically, a means of placing electronic files in a shared location where they can be easily accessed by other people working on the same *project*

I

inbetweens – the *frames* that connect between major points of a motion

ink and paint – the process of using these tools to create and color *2D animation* (either *cel* or *Flash*) by applying information in the *color keys* (or *color mark-ups*)

K

keyframe – a *3D animation* process where only the most important movements are *animated* and a computer program determines the needed *inbetweens* and generates them

L

layout – a drawing for how a place in an *animated project* storyline looks (see also *background* or *location*)

leica reel – an alternate term used by some studios to refer to what is more commonly known as an *animatic* (see *animatic*)

legal – the area of a project that deals with *contracts, clearances,* etc. (see also *business affairs*)

limited animation – the process by which the same *frame* of *animation* appears twice in a row for each movement; the *fps* is still fast enough to create the illusion of motion

lip assign – the process of using a *mouth chart* to record *character* mouth movements on an *exposure sheet* (*x-sheet*); action is handled separately by

a *sheet timer*

lip sync – the process of mouth movements of the *characters* to the *dialogue*

live-action – in contrast to *animation,* these are *productions* involving the use of human actors instead of drawn figures; sometimes, live-action material can be used to create animation (see *rotoscoping*)

location – an area where an *animated project* takes place (see also *background* or *layout*)

M

M&E – Music and Effects; refers to the final *mix* of these *elements* blended onto a single track of the finished *animated project*

main model pack – the standard *models* that will be used throughout the life of a *project*

marketing – getting the word out that a *film* or *series* is available to be viewed

mentoring – giving assistance to someone else to help them grow in their career or as an individual

mix – the process of blending together the *dialogue, music,* and *effects* track with the *animation*

model – a drawing that indicates how a *character, prop,* or *background* should look in order to maintain consistency

model sheet – a form with standardized labeling to help organize the various *character, prop,* or *background* elements

motion capture – a process where actors wear suits containing sensors at key movement points and have their motions captured on camera; these motions are later loaded into the computer and applied to *animated characters*

mouth chart – a set of drawings indicating how a character looks when speaking various phonetic sounds; this information is then translated during *lip assign* to the *exposure sheets* (*x-sheets*)

multiplane camera – a special device used to take pictures of *cel animation* layers

N

network – a specific means of *exhibition* that can be viewed in people's homes

networking – the process of getting together with and meeting other professionals

non-union – a *project* not protected by any collective bargaining unit in one or more production areas

normal pause edit – a compilation of the best *circle takes,* edited together at regular intervals

O

outline – a *scene* by scene "map" of the major points in a story

outsourcing – sending work to *animation* houses elsewhere in the country or world

overseas supervisor – someone on the payroll of the *project* who stays full-time on-site at an *outsourcing* location

P

panel – a single picture in a *storyboard*

paste up – the process of putting *models* on *model sheets*

polygon – in *3D animation,* a general term for the basic shapes that make up a *rendered* element

post production – the stages of making a *project* after it undergoes the *shipping* process to the *animation* house and is returned as *footage*

premise – a one to three line summary of a *feature* or *episode* idea

pre-production – the stages of making a *project* before it undergoes the *shipping* process to the *animation* house

prime-time – in contrast to *daytime* animation, this term is used specifically to refer to programs intended primarily for an adult audience

producer – generally, someone who oversees an *animated project,* though there are many levels for this position

production – a term used to described the stage when the actual *animation* is being drawn and then recorded to *film stock* or *video*

project – a piece of *animation* (e.g., *episode, feature*)

prop – an item used by a *character*

R

reading – a *voice actor's* performance of *dialogue*

recording – the process of capturing the *voice actors'* performances for use in the *project*

reference pack – an optional resource detailing items such as preferred *storyboard* staging, the use of light and shadow, etc. (see also *style guide*)

render – in *3D animation,* a term used to describe building an *element* in the computer

resolution – in *3D animation,* refers to detail level of the animation; it can be either low (minimal detail) or high (fully detailed)

retake – the redoing of one or more *scenes* due to either, either on the part of the *project* or of the *outsourcing* company

rights – the legal ownership of any creative work (including *bible, script,* or completed *film* or *series*)

rotoscoping – a process of tracing *live-action* footage to create *animation*

rough storyboard – a series of *sequences* that emphasize staging and cinematography over accuracy of *characters, props,* etc.

S

scene – a set of *storyboard panels* with a consistent camera angle or perspective

scheduling – determining how long it will take to do each phase of a *project*

script – a written guideline for the *storyboard* and *animation* to follow in telling the *story*

sequel – a follow-up *story* (usually to a *feature*) including the same characters as the prior *project*

sequence – a set of *scenes* taking place in the same location

series – a group of *episodes* (usually for *television*)

session – examples include a *recording* or *mix* session

sheet timer – someone who records *character* movement information on *exposure sheets* (*x-sheets*); mouth movement is handled by a separate person dedicated to *lip assign*

shipping – packing up all the relevant *elements* and sending them to an *outsourcing* location

shorts – see *short film*

short film – a *film* of short duration, in animation usually less than 70 minutes in length and often five minutes or less

size comparison – placing *characters* side by side to show their relative heights

special pose or costume – a way that a *character* dresses or looks that is not how the *character* usually appears

staff – in contrast to *freelance,* someone who works at the office and is on company payroll

stock – *elements* that can easily be reused

Stop-Motion animation – the process of using figurines (most commonly clay, but others are possible) and shooting them *frame* by frame to create an illusion of motion

story – the journey the *characters* go through that becomes the basis for the *animation*

storyboard – a series of *panels* often based on a *script* that provide a visual blueprint for the *animation*

style guide – an optional resource detailing items such as preferred *storyboard* staging, the use of light and shadow, etc. (see also *reference pack*)

symbol library – a term specific to *Flash animation* as to how it stores its *stock* materials in the computer

T

table read – usually done only in *prime-time animation* or *live-action*, this process involves the *voice actors* sitting and reading lines for practice and for the *writers* to see if any rewriting is required

target audience – the group of people a *project* hopes to reach (see *demographics*)

teleconference – the use of audio technology for multiple people to share ideas (compare to *videoconference*)

theater – a place of *exhibition* for *animated film*

timing – the process of figuring out how long in screen time it takes a certain action to occur

title sequence – designed to set the look, tone, and feel of a *project* and used at the start and the end of the piece

track reader – someone who translates the *normal pause edit* into phonetic sound that then requires *lip assign* to match it to the respective *mouth chart*

U

union – An organization that represents the interests of a select group of individuals involved in a production. Examples of unions in the United States include The Animation Guild 839, the Screen Actors Guild, and the Writers Guild of America

V

vectorization – in *Flash animation*, the ability for multiple steps to be done at once

vehicle – a specific kind of *prop* used for the transportation of *characters*

video – what animation transfers to when each frame is captured digitally from a source

videoconference – the use of audiovisual technology for multiple people to share information (compare to *teleconference*)

voice actor – someone who provides the voice for a *character* in an *animated project*

W

work print – a rough copy of completed *animation* for evaluation purposes in the *post-production* process

work-for-hire – employment on a *project* where the end result is owned by someone else (i.e., the hired party gets no creative stake)

wrap party – a celebration of the
conclusion of a *project*
writer – someone who crafts the *story*

X

x-sheets – A shorthand term for
exposure sheets (see *exposure sheets*)

ACKNOWLEDGEMENTS

To my family, for always believing.

To Kevin Paul Shaw Broden, love of my life, and his family for being there when my family could not.

To Marc Handler, Christy Marx, and Greg Weisman, for being incredible beacons of professional and personal wisdom to light the path that brought me here.

To Larry DiTillio, for letting someone he'd never met in person (but with references!) housesit for two weeks and figure out if she could survive Los Angeles or not.

To George Chialtis for teaching Introduction to Animation Timing at Nickelodeon, to give me a richer understanding of how the process works.

To all the professionals who gave their time to be part of this book goes a very special thank you, as to all those who gave me a chance to work alongside them over the years.

In memory of Katherine Lawrence and Dr. David K. Terwische ("Dr. Dave").

INDEX

H

Handler, Marc 25, 203
Hanna-Barbera 18, 82, 126
He-Man and the Masters of the Universe 32, 96, 100
Heavy Metal 2000/ FAKK 2 100
Hellboy 4, 5
Hellboy Animated 4, 5
Hercules 4, 190
hi-res 154
high polygon models 152
Hornswiggle 178
Hulk 1, The 100
Hulk 2, The 100
Hunchback of Notre Dame II, The 107
Hunchback of Notre Dame, The 107, 126

I

IATSE 17
inbetweens 157, 158, 198
industry networking seminars 75
inker 150
interpreter 105
Invader Zim 92
involvement barriers 117
Iron Giant, The 126

J

Jem and the Holograms 32
Johnson, Carl 107
Jumanji 130
Jungle Software 83

K

keyframe 157, 198
kill 33, 94, 117
Kim Possible 34, 67
Kinofilm 92, 93
Koepnick, Bill 170

L

layout artist 98
layout artists 132
Legend of Prince Valiant, The 190
Legend of Zelda, The 96
leica reel 103, 136, 143, 147, 195, 198
Liberty's Kids 190
Lightwave 151
limited animation 82, 198
line producer 3, 6, 7, 8, 9, 92, 94, 158
line producers 7, 92
lip assign 104, 198, 199, 200, 201
lip sync 125, 143, 144, 146, 157, 169, 197, 198
live-action 8, 18, 30, 32, 45, 49, 61, 125, 147, 190, 198, 200, 201
live-action script 30
live-action sitcom script 61
lo-res 154
loglines 41
low polygon models 152

M

M&E (see also Music and Effects) 24, 172, 198
main model pack 98, 130, 198
Make Way for Noddy 84
marketing 16, 34, 177, 179, 180, 181, 182, 183, 185, 186, 189, 198
Martin Mystery 100
Marx, Christy 32, 203
mass mailing 181
master shots 30
Max Steel 67, 84, 100, 160
Maya 151
Media Services 83
mentoring 191, 198
MGM Animation 96
Mighty Ducks, The 107
Mike, Lu, & Og 92
mini-bible 75
MIP 75, 85

mix 31, 168, 171, 172, 198, 200
model sheet 99, 127, 135, 198
model sheets 99, 105, 124, 127, 135, 144, 146, 150, 199
motion capture 157, 199
Motion Picture Screen Cartoonists Guild 18
mouth chart 104, 130, 157, 198, 199, 201
Movie Magic Budgeting 83
Movie Magic Scheduling 83
Movie Magic Screenwriter 30
MPSC. *See also Motion Picture Screen Cartoonists Guild*
Mucha Lucha 100, 158
music and effects (M&E) 24, 172, 198
My Little Pony 84, 100

N

Nagel, Jan 181
NATPE 85
network 4, 18, 65, 84, 146, 179, 182, 197, 199
New Generation Pictures 67
Nickelodeon 18, 86, 92, 158, 178, 203
Noddy 84, 100, 103, 154, 157, 173
non-union 17, 18, 19, 27, 103, 199
normal pause edit 102, 104, 125, 135, 143, 144, 146, 168, 195, 199, 201

O

Oh Yeah! Cartoon 182
Olsen, Jimmy 5
outline 10, 31, 45, 49, 65, 66, 72, 76, 199
outline stage 65, 76
outsourcing 75, 113, 115, 116, 117, 118, 199, 200
overseas studio 81, 132
overseas supervisor 105, 116, 117, 149, 159, 160, 161, 164, 199

P

panel 65, 99, 104, 136, 137, 199
paste up 135, 199
PayMaster 84
pencil test 150, 151
permission 16
Pet Alien 160
Piglet's Big Movie 107
Pinky and the Brain 107
pitches 27, 41, 74, 94
plotline 41, 46
polygon 113, 152, 153, 154, 155, 156, 199
Pooh's Grand Adventure 107
post production 135, 151, 199
post-production dialogue editor 106
potential investor 75
potentiometer 102
premise 34, 41, 42, 45, 49, 72, 199
Prikryl, Josh 160
primary audience 74
prime-time 18, 30, 37, 41, 61, 196, 199, 201
prime-time animation script 30, 61
production assistant 103
production coordinators xii, 102, 103
production manager 7-9, 94, 158

prop designer 99
props 11, 45, 46, 97-99, 105, 123, 127, 130, 133-136, 145, 147, 150, 162, 195, 198, 200-201

R

Rainbow Fish 190
Random Cartoon 178
reading xii, 10, 30, 41, 101, 125, 143, 196, 200, 201
Reboot 32, 100
recording session dialogue editor 102
recording session engineer 102
Reel Logix 83

Reel Production Calendar 83
reference pack 135, 200, 201
render 152, 154, 200
Rescuers, The 4
residuals 18, 19
resolution 113, 154, 200
retake 81, 106, 113, 131, 162, 168, 169, 200
Return of Jafar 4, 107
rights ii, 16, 19, 27, 31, 45, 96, 172, 188, 196, 200
Robot Chicken 146
Rocket Power 34
rotoscoping 146, 150, 157, 198, 200
rough cut 165, 185
rough storyboard 97, 136, 147, 200
Roughnecks: The Starship Troopers Chronicles 41, 67
Royal Navy, The 190
Rugrats 34

S

Scary Godmother 100
Schwartz, Sander 12
scratch track 126
Screen Actors Guild 19, 201
script breakdown 124, 127
script coordinator 95
Scriptware 30
scriptwriters 29
SD Entertainment 84, 96
Search and Rescue 190
segment producer 8
segment type 8
self-contained episodes 72
sense of scale 130, 134
sequel 16, 65, 66, 114, 188, 200
sequence 137, 138, 139, 140, 141, 142, 145, 160, 200, 201
series bible 34, 41, 42, 72
Shadow of Rome 126
Shadow Raiders 100
She-Ra 96, 114
sheet timer 104, 143, 144, 198, 200

short film 179, 200
shorts 123, 182, 200
shot calls 49
show bible 34, 37
Showbiz Budgeting 83
Showbiz Labor Guide 84
Showbiz RateMaster 84
sides 11, 13, 124, 125
Simpsons, The 61
size comparison 130, 131, 133, 134, 200
sluggers 104
software programs 72
Sonic the Hedgehog 96
Sony Animation 12, 92
South Park 85
spec 31
special characters and poses 99
special post 128, 195, 200
speculation 31, 45
Spider-Man 190
Spike & Mike 179
Spongebob Squarepants 65
springboards 41
staff writers 94
Static Shock 190
stock 98, 151, 197, 199, 200, 201
Stones, Tad 4
stop-motion animation 91, 146, 147, 195, 200
story editor 94
storyboard artists 29, 97, 98, 99, 100, 132, 135, 136, 147, 159
storyboard stage 10, 132
storyboard supervisor 97, 136
storypersons 18
Studio B 85
style guide 135, 200, 201
Superfriends 126
supervising producer. *See also* line producer
supervisory producer 8
symbol library 158, 201